SEVEN BIBLE MYSTERIES YOU MAY HAVE
MISSED THAT WILL CHANGE YOUR LIFE

CONNECTING
the DOTS

D1637042

GENE BINDER

HIGHERLIFE
PUBLISHING & MARKETING

Connecting the Dots: Seven Bible Mysteries You May Have Missed That Will Change Your Life

Publisher:
HigherLife Publishing and Marketing
PO Box 623307
Oviedo, FL 32762

Copyright, © 2017 Gene Binder

All rights reserved. No part of this book may be reproduced in any form, except for brief quotations in reviews, without the written permission of the author.

Printed in the United States of America. All rights reserved under International Copyright Law.

ISBN 978-0-9989773-6-2

Library of Congress Control Number: 1-5766174681

Scripture quotations are taken from THE HOLY BIBLE, NEW INTERNATIONAL VERSION®, NIV® Copyright © 1973, 1978, 1984, 2011 by Biblica, Inc.™ Used by permission of Zondervan. All rights reserved worldwide. www.zondervan.com The "NIV" and "New International Version" are trademarks registered in the United States Patent and Trademark Office by Biblica, Inc.™

When marked as ESV, Scripture quotations are from the ESV® Bible (The Holy Bible, English Standard Version®), copyright © 2001 by Crossway, a publishing ministry of Good News Publishers. Used by permission. All rights reserved worldwide.

Table of Contents

INTRODUCTION

Sleep has never come easy for me. I am naturally an energetic person who has a flurry of ideas racing around my head that don't seem to submit to the fatigue of my body. It is not unusual for me to wander the house late into the night or early into the morning. My staff gives me a hard time about the "time stamps" on the emails that I send which verify my bout with insomnia. But over a decade ago there was a night that was different from my usual restlessness. I awoke around 1:00 a.m., which was late or early…even for me. I felt alert and a sense of purpose, like God was wanting to speak to me and this was His appointed meeting hour. I went downstairs trying not to wake up my sleeping wife and began to pray.

In my history as a follower of Yeshua I have only heard God speak with almost audible clarity a couple of times. Yet in the darkness of the early hours, I heard the word FORESHADOWS. I quickly opened my Bible and searched for references that would illuminate the word reverberating around my mind, but to no avail. So I did what any good Bible student would do—I broke down the word. How about the word "shadow"? From that point on, the search was on and my life would never be the same.

I never made it back to bed that night, and for hours I studied The Word like never before. I felt like the two disciples on the road to Emmaus as the hidden, but very Risen Messiah, unlocked the mysteries of the scriptures. The Lord set up appointments like this one for the next four consecutive nights to follow.

What happened over five sleepless days shifted my life calling, my ministry, and eventually my church. The book you hold in your hands is the fruit that was planted deep in my soul that night. It has taken almost fifteen years to get these words onto the pages of this book, but the message was too important to rush. It needed to be lived out in my life and then pruned in the context of a local congregation in Boulder, Colorado. I am forever grateful and humbled that God woke me up from my slumber that fateful night to reveal His Foreshadow story.

Connecting The Dots unveils the eternal plan of the God who was, is, and is to come.

So, while I take no credit for the material in this book, I want to emphasize this information is extraordinary. *Connecting The Dots* will transform the often complex, mystifying nature of the Bible into a simple, understandable, and beautiful love story. You will see how God's story is seamless and purposeful from beginning to end as all the puzzle pieces fall into place. Even more importantly, you will clearly see how your story fits into God's story.

The concepts presented in *Connecting The Dots* are a collection of astonishing previews, which cumulatively unveil God's master plan unfolding through the ages. Each successive foreshadow deals with what God is ultimately planning to do at a later stage of human history. Some of the foreshadowed events have partially occurred, whereas others are yet unfolding. In summation, *Connecting The Dots* unveils the eternal plan of the God who was, is, and is to come.

In my opinion, one of the greatest movie trilogies of all time is Peter Jackson's, *The Lord of the Rings*. The concept is based on

J.R.R. Tolkien's epic book by the same name. Both the book and the three films—*The Fellowship of The Ring, The Two Towers, and The Return of the King*—tell the story of a heavily burdened hobbit laden with problems that go beyond his everyday expertise. He sets out on a very un-hobbit-like quest, and encounters all sorts of strange beings and creatures along the way, including a few representatives of humankind. The story is full of adventure and romance, and explores the nature of both good and evil. Movie trilogies like Jackson's are meant to be absorbed in their entirety and in chronological order. If you only watch the first episode, *The Fellowship of The Ring*, the story will have no resolution. On the other hand, if you only watch the final episode, *The Return of the King*, the story has no context. I presume Jackson would shudder at the thought of someone trying to experience the fullness of the tale Tolkien wove without engaging in all three films.

Those sleepless nights in 2004, the Lord revealed how the Bible is also a trilogy. Like any trilogy, the Bible is meant to be absorbed in its entirety and in chronological order. In keeping with all great stories, God has written an amazing love story filled with romance and adventure, mysterious twists and turns, and nail-biting suspense. The many books and chapters embedded within this great story continue escalating to reach a powerful climax. In this climax, the Hero of the story carries out a supremely bold and daring mission to rescue His lover, who has been taken captive by an archetypal villain.

At several junctures within God's story it appears as though the Hero is failing in His quest. In the end, His plan ultimately succeeds. After the quintessential villain is permanently defeated, the lovers are reunited in our favorite, heart-warming scene—the couple rides off together into the sunset to live happily ever after.

While it may sound like a great medieval legend, this is certainly no make-believe story. This is the real deal. The God of the Bible wrote this story, which is undoubtedly the greatest love story ever told. Because all humans are made in the image and likeness of God, every other hero story conceived or imagined is merely a smaller version of this all-encompassing story written by God. His story is embedded in our DNA, whether we believe in God or not. God's complete story actually precedes time as we know it and is meant to be absorbed from beginning to end.

Through the prophet Isaiah, the Bible expresses a similar sentiment, explaining in detail God's master plan unfolding through time:

> *"Remember the former things, those of long ago; I am God, and there is no other; I am God, and there is none like me. I make known the end from the beginning, from ancient times, what is still to come. I say: My purpose will stand, and I will do all that I please. From the east I summon a bird of prey; from a far-off land, a man to fulfill my purpose. What I have said, that will I bring about; what I have planned, that will I do"* *(Isaiah 46:9-11).*

Notice how this passage clearly depicts how God's story will unfold, page by page, exactly the way He wrote it. It also points to a certain fact—nothing can stop the unfolding of this story through time. With this in mind, *Connecting The Dots* will demonstrate how this astounding story fits together into one perfect and purposeful account, unfolding in a thrilling trilogy of three very dramatic episodes.

WHAT IS *CONNECTING THE DOTS* ALL ABOUT?

Have you ever wondered what God's purpose was in giving us the blueprint of His plan? The answer that He wants us to know His heart, His mind, and where we fit into His plan. This is why

God selected a range of human beings to write the Bible under His inspiration. The various foreshadows contained within God's biblical blueprint are units of meaning that help to unveil God's eternal plan—units of meaning that unveil God's purpose, which is to establish an eternal family. We are currently racing towards the end of the story, after which we will start afresh with a new beginning. I believe many people will be astounded at who the Lord is going to use in the leading role to wrap up the story. *Connecting The Dots* allows us to see the Bible as one beautiful, adventure-packed love story from beginning to end. These "foreshadows " unveil how the dots are connected throughout all three dramatic episodes. Because God wrote this love story, we can be assured it will unfold in alignment with His prediction. It will take many nail-biting twists and turns before His goal to establish an eternal family is finally accomplished. We are firsthand witnesses experiencing the harrowing events taking place across the globe, which you will come to see are the culmination of foreshadowed events. When you are familiar with the concept of foreshadowing, you recognize the unfolding of God's master plan even when you read some global headlines. I will explain more on this later.

So, what is the core of *Connecting The Dots*? We will examine seven prophetic pictures portraying God's unbreakable covenant relationship with Israel and how that relates to current and end times. The first episode of this thrilling trilogy establishes God's covenant relationship with His chosen nation. God is faithful and will one day fulfill all his covenantal promises to Israel, however, as a foreshadow this leads into the second episode, in which Israel find their messianic fulfillment. In the third and final episode, God's covenant people become eternally completed in a place the Bible calls, "New Jerusalem."

These are the seven foreshadows in their logical progressive chronological order:

The First foreshadow: "The Covenant"—in short, the

covenant is God's marriage to Israel. When you have a marriage, children usually follow. This leads us to the next foreshadow.

The Second foreshadow: "The Nation of Israel"—this is the family. When a family has been established, a home becomes essential. This leads to the next foreshadow.

The Third foreshadow is: "The Promised Land"—this is the family home. When in a home, every good family has to have a healthy set of rules which, yet again, takes us to the next foreshadow.

The Fourth foreshadow is: "The Torah (law)"—these are the rules by which the family abide, the family law. Balancing the family rules, all healthy families need to have a foundational aspect of virtue—Dad has to be present and accessible to the children. This leads to the next foreshadow.

The Fifth foreshadow is: "The Temple"—this is the means by which the children have access to their Father. Every wise father provides plenty of easy access for his kids to approach him. This leads to the next foreshadow. Special times of fellowship must be set aside, leading to the penultimate foreshadow.

The Sixth foreshadow is: "The Sabbath"—also known

in Hebrew as Shabbat, this is the time set apart to cease from work for one day. Everyone needs a day of rest to focus on what is really important, each week for the family to be together. All healthy families need quality time away from the drudgery of everyday life, leading to the seventh and final foreshadow.

The Seventh foreshadow is: "The Feasts"—these are a series of seven major annual family gatherings set in a mix of spiritual and agrarian observances. The feasts are probably the most spectacular of all, in foreshadowing the Messiah.

THE SEVEN FORESHADOWS	
The Covenant the marriage	**The Temple** access to dad
The Nation of Israel the family	**The Sabbath** family rest
The Promised Land the family home	**The Feasts** family gatherings
The Law the family rules	

Together, these seven foreshadows reveal the eternal plan of the God who was, is, and is to come, and as well as His plan to establish an eternal family. What makes these foreshadows truly fascinating is the manner in which they all follow a three-phase progressive pattern within God's trilogy. Each foreshadow will be examined in detail as we progress through the chapters.

A useful insight to bear in mind is that each foreshadow is built on the foundation of God's trilogy-like sacred name, as defined by the Hebrew characters יהוה—YHVH or Yod-Hey-Vav-Hey. The Hebrew expression of this name translates into three aspects of linear time: the God who was—relative to the first episode of prophetic pictures; the God who is—relative to the second episode, in which Israel find their messianic fulfillment; and the God who will be—relative to the third and final episode of eternal completion in New Jerusalem. The Book of Revelation states it this way: "Holy, holy, holy is the Lord God Almighty, who was [the first episode], and is [the second episode], and is to come [episode three]" (Rev. 4:8).

Connecting The Dots will also demonstrate how the Jewish people play a leading role in this story, throughout history, to the present day, and even beyond. My prayer is that *Connecting The Dots* will build your faith and inspire your heart in ways you have never experienced before. I pray these cumulative foreshadows help you to see God's complete story, perhaps for the first time. Even more importantly, I pray you recognize your own personal story in relation to these Biblical foreshadows—I hope you come to realize God has written your story, too. Consider what the psalmist had to say: "...All the days ordained for me were written in Your book before one of them came to be" (Psa. 139:16).

You might ask, "So God enters my days into some kind of book?" Yes, it is called, "*The Greatest Story Ever Written*," and I hope, as we continue, you will see how your story—the one God wrote for you personally—is woven into this bigger story. There really is nothing better than to awaken to this truth.

The primary question is, "Why isn't everyone aware of this profound story?" Well, I think of it like those 3D glasses you wear when you watch a 3D movie because you need a special pair of glasses to read between the lines of God's trilogy. How else will you be able to connect the dots between the three episodes of God's trilogy? Let us begin by seeing how to access and use these special glasses.

PART I

CHAPTER 1

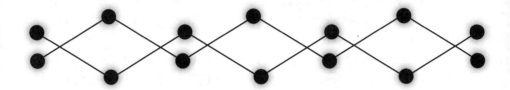

Seeing the Whole Story

ave you ever been to a movie shown in 3D, where you have to wear special glasses? I love 3D movies because you get an extra depth of experience to the film. God's story works the same way. We need special glasses, too, to help us see and understand the true depth of the story. Imagine in God's trilogy you have the option of wearing one of three pairs of special reading glasses. To recognize which pair is needed to see this trilogy as one seamless, purposeful story from beginning to end, let's imagine the choices are Jewish glasses, Christian glasses, or Jewish-Christian glasses. While wearing only the Jewish glasses, God's story would be alive with meaning, but you would not fully understand and embrace the hopeful Messianic future that unfolds during the second episode. Nor would you easily comprehend how this first episode is finally completed during the third episode. You would have no resolution, and it would be easy to become stuck in the details of the first episode.

When reading God's story, wearing only the Christian glasses, you would appreciate the detail of this episode, as well as new details of the first episode, but you would not thoroughly understand the full impact the first episode has on the second and third episodes. In this instance, you would have no context and would easily veer off track when trying to comprehend the entire story. The only way to fully appreciate and understand God's trilogy is when you wear Jewish-Christian glasses. These glasses allow us to connect the dots between all the episodes. They give us a complete picture of the whole story.

When you wear these special "Jewish-Christian glasses," you not only begin to see God's story in brilliant three-dimensional awe and wonder, you also know exactly where you are in the story. This is essential, because when you know where you are in God's story, you can recognize how your story intersects into God's larger story. You begin to understand your purpose and what you're supposed to do. As we embark together on this incredible journey called *Connecting The Dots*, you will need a Bible that contains the whole story, not just episode one or episode two, but the complete trilogy.

GOD ETERNAL

Given a preview of God's trilogy, we see the story begins in eternity past and ends in eternity future. We learned that God is eternal. He has no beginning and He has no end. God has always existed, and He will always exist. Moreover, God's story is filled with this teaching about His eternal existence. The first episode of the story from the *Tanakh*, the Hebrew scriptures, gives us an example of God's most sacred and unpronounceable name. This name consists of four Hebrew letters: יהוה, pronounced as Yod-Hey-Vav-Hey. This is essentially a contraction of the verb "to be" or "to exist." *Yod-Hey-Vav-Hey* contains past, present, and future language features, and so in this one mysterious word, God describes Himself as the God who was, and is, and who will be. These are the deep details encompassed in this one word. It is a description of God's eternal being before, through, and beyond time.

Speaking through the prophet, Isaiah, God said, "...I am the first and I am the last; apart from me there is no other God" (Isa. 44:6). The very same sentiment is expressed in the second episode of God's trilogy, spoken in the New Testament by Jesus: "I am the Alpha and the Omega, the First and the Last, the Beginning and the End" (Rev. 22:13). These verses say that no one created God. This information causes a short-circuit in our human mind. Because to say God has always existed is one thing, but when we try to conceive of someone existing even though He was not created, we simply draw a blank. It is usually better not to go there unless you want smoke pouring out of your ears.

God existed before time began and God will exist after time ends. God lives outside of time. He is eternally existent.

God existed before time began and God will exist after time ends. God lives outside of time. He is eternally existent. You and I, however, are stuck in time. We cannot run away from the clock. It is always ticking. We are stuck here for the time being.

The first verse in the first chapter of Genesis begins with the Hebrew phrase "בְּרֵאשִׁית בָּרָא אֱלֹהִים," pronounced phonetically "*Bereshit Bara Elohim...*" These words translate into English as, "In the beginning God created..." This phrase explicitly clarifies that before anything material existed in the universe—just prior to a major historical event called, "The Beginning"—God already existed in eternity past. At some point before this historical event we call, "The Beginning," God decided to create something outside of eternity, and consequently, history and time began. Think of Genesis 1:1 as God pressing the play button on history, marking the beginning of the whole story.

With the launch of episode one, the rave reviews started rolling in: "Insightful and inspiring, a brilliant tale of love," says Rotten Tomatoes. "Mysterious awe and wonder, with plenty of twists and turns," says Roger Ebert. "An absolute game-changer," according to *The New York Times.*

As numerous Bible passages inform us, both time and history not only have a beginning, but also have an eventual end. Another way to understand this is to recognize our flawed and currently imperfect history will eventually arrive at a new beginning, presenting us with an unflawed future. This is normally the way all hero stories eventually arrive at their ending. When we see the words, "The End," scrolling across the screen, it's just the beginning of a great new future. When we're left to imagine the scene following, "The End," we create an image of this rosy new future in our minds' eye. We follow a story where things start off well, but then all of a sudden dark music starts playing, and the nefarious villain shows up. Then, throughout the story, the hero arrives, saves the day, and the main characters ride off into the sunset. The End. But is it the end? Well, actually, no because we imagine the main characters have a great new future ahead of them wherein they live happily ever-after.

The prophet Isaiah wrote about this new beginning: "Behold, I will create new heavens and a new earth. The former things will not be remembered, nor will they come to mind" (Isa. 65:17). He goes on to describe a world free of conflict, pain, and suffering. The Book of Revelation has this passage from Isaiah in view when it states, "Then I saw a new heaven and a new earth, for the first heaven and the first earth had passed away..." (Rev. 21:1). This description in Revelation also describes the same peaceful, paradise-like world mentioned by Isaiah, where there is no pain, no suffering, no sorrow, and not even death. In the first beginning, God created the universe we currently live in, where time and history began to click off units of time like the counter of a video player—which is still clicking off these units of time. He started by creating the heavens, moved onto creating the Earth, and then created everything living on the Earth.

IS THERE ONLY *ONE* GOD?

The Hebrew word for God in the opening passage of Genesis is the word, *Elohim*, which is the plural form of the word "God." *Eloah* is the singular form of the word "God," which is used frequently in the Hebrew Bible, and is almost always used as a reference to the God of Israel. To make sense of this, we have to ask ourselves the question, "Why would God choose to introduce Himself for the very first time in the plural, rather than the singular?"

Imagine if, when introducing myself, I said, "Hi, I'm Genes." It would be grammatically incorrect and possibly funny. Similarly, we might just dismiss God's plural introduction as a stylistic type of Hebraic prose—which some people actually do. When we reach verse twenty-six, we discover another plural oddity. This passage of scripture, yet again, refers to God in the plural form: "Then God (Elohim) said, 'Let us make man in our image...'" (Gen. 1:26). Did you catch that? Let *us* make man in *our* image.

Who exactly is God having a conversation with in this passage of scripture? Who could possibly be on an equal level to Him, especially in a creative sense? And why does God declare over and over again throughout the Bible that He alone is God, and there is no one else like Him? I'm Jewish, and Jews believe there is only one God. The reason we believe there is only one God is because our Hebrew Bible—the first episode of God's story—repeatedly informs us there is only one God. In every Synagogue service, every week, we recite what we call *The Shema*, from Deuteronomy 6:4: "*Shema Israel: Adonai Elohainu, Adonai*

Echad," translated as, "Hear, O Israel: the Lord our God, the Lord is One."

In truth, there is only *one* God. The moment your theology claims there is more than one God, you know you've stumbled off the path. Some people do lose track of this truth, most likely because they don't have a solid grasp of the context from episode one. We do have to ask ourselves the question, "If there is only one God, why would God use a plural noun to describe Himself, especially in the context of introducing Himself to the world for the very first time?" And why, just a few verses later, would He say, "Let us make man in our image"—if there is only one God?

The answer to this question requires those special Jewish-Christian glasses that enable us to comprehend the complete trilogy. Let's put those glasses on for a moment to make sense of why this one God uses a plural pronoun to refer to Himself. The first episode of God's trilogy begins in a very serene garden. God creates Adam and Eve, and places them in this garden. It's a garden of great delights, an idyllic paradise where both the first man and the first woman are intimately connected to their God, and each other. Almost immediately, an obstacle arises. Dark, sinister music is cued, and a sly, slithering serpent winds his way between the couple and their loving God. Satan tempts Eve with the illusion of independence and she and her husband, Adam, are deceived by the diabolical villain. Adam and Eve sin, causing themselves to be separated from God and from each other. They are both expelled from the security and the comfort of their perfect paradise. This is a pivotal point in the story, as the action accelerates rapidly from this juncture. The rest of the story starts unfolding as God initiates a daring rescue plan to bring all of humankind back into an intimate relationship, not only with Himself, but with each other.

Not surprisingly, God's rescue plan involves a Superhero. The Hebrew Bible calls Him the *Mashiach*, the Messiah, the Savior who will save the day and make everything right in the world again. The Bible continually references this Superhero throughout the first episode of God's trilogy. This passage, written by the prophet, Micah, is one of many references to God's promised Superhero: "But you, Bethlehem Ephrathah, though you are small among the clans of Judah, out of you will come for me one who will be ruler over Israel, whose origins are from of old, from ancient times" (Micah 5:2—A footnote says, "Or from days of eternity").

What is fascinating about this particular messianic passage is the timeframe allocated to the Superhero. His origins are from ancient times or from days of eternity. Micah lived several thousand years ago and wrote this passage in a period of history currently considered ancient. The question then becomes, *just how ancient is this Superhero that Micah describes?* Micah brings to our attention that this messianic Superhero previously existed (from days of eternity) before He arrived to save the day. How is it possible for our Superhero to have existed before He has arrived? When we put on our special, Jewish-Christian glasses, everything becomes clear. We can easily recognize Micah is alluding to the fact this Superhero existed before the beginning of time.

When we read John's gospel, Micah's allusion to the Superhero existing before the beginning of time make sense. This is how John explains it:

> *"In the beginning was the Word, and the Word was with God, and the Word was God. He was with God in the beginning. Through him all things were made; without him nothing was made that has been made"* *(John 1:1-3).*

Does this passage really say, "the Word was God," and if so, who is the Word? Yes, John tells us the Word was God, and as we keep reading the balance of John's first chapter, we realize he is referring to *Yeshua* as the Word. Jesus is the Word. The passage informs us Jesus was with God in the beginning, and through Him—through whom? Through Jesus.

Through Jesus all things were made. Without Him nothing was made that has been made. John's gospel starts in a similar way to the Book of Genesis: In the beginning—and the mention of the Word in this passage obviously refers to Jesus, who was not only there creating with God in the beginning—*but is, in fact, God.* As we continue reading the first chapter of John's gospel, we are informed, "The Word became flesh and made his dwelling among us" (John 1:14).

How does this all fit together? According to Genesis in the first episode, God presents Himself in the plural form (Elohim) in the beginning. The creation process was started in the beginning, and according to Genesis 1:26, God was co-creating with at least one other equal. Micah later informs us the Superhero in this story has eternal origins. We then fast-forward to the second episode, in which John tells us it was none other than Yeshua (Jesus) creating with God in the beginning. Given this overview, it becomes clear who at least one other person co-creating with God actually is (let us make man in our image). He is Jesus, who is, in fact, God who became flesh and dwelled among us.

Now, don't take those special Jewish-Christian glasses off just yet. There is another question to ask, a question summarizing all the details discussed so far: We know there is only one God, so could it be that this God who describes Himself in the plural form and this promised Superhero whose origins are from eternity past are really one and the same person?

Is it possible this God who describes Himself in a plural form is both the Creator and the Messiah? Remember, God personally wrote this beautiful love story, so could it be that He is the Author, the Director, and the Star of the greatest story ever told? A story where God breaks into our world as a humble man so He can rescue us from the diabolical villain by shedding His own blood to make atonement for our sins? If this is the case, why do so many people find it difficult to believe?

MASKS AND BLINDERS

Perhaps another popular film, *The Mark of Zorro*[1], will help to shed some light on this question. In this story, an ordinary man named Don Diego de la Vega and a valiant superhero named Zorro are really the same person. However, nobody realizes this crucial fact, not even the heroine of the movie. Nobody knows because whenever Don Diego becomes Zorro, he wears a silly little mask. Don Diego is right there for everyone to see, but the mask he wears blinds everyone from seeing who he really is.

Similar to the friends of Zorro being unable to recognize Don Diego, because of his mask, a verse from the second episode of God's story gives us some insight concerning why people struggle to recognize the Creator God and the Messiah God being one and the same: "The god of this age [meaning Satan] has blinded the minds of unbelievers, so that they cannot see the light of the gospel of the glory of Christ [Messiah], who is the image of God" (2 Cor. 4:4).

I can personally vouch for the phenomenon of being blinded to this reality. I walked into a church for the first time a little over thirty-three years ago. Yes, there I was, a Jewish man going to church. Yet, something profound happened to me that day, and it changed the course of my life forever. On that day, the blinders fell off my eyes. For the first time in my life, the truth was unveiled. I saw the truth in my Hebrew Bible, a Bible I had read often as a child. My Hebrew Bible was filled with clear messages of our God (Elohim) being both God the Author of the story, and God the Hero of the story. But for some reason I could not see it clearly until I was in my thirties. It was there right in front of me the en-

---

1 Foote, John Taintor, Garrett Fort, Bess Meredyth, Johnston McCulley, The Mark of Zorro. Directed by Rouben Mamoulian. Los Angeles: Twentieth Century Fox Film Corporation, 1940.

tire time, but the god of this age, the devil, had blinded me from this reality for thirty-three years. Thankfully, thirty-three years ago, the God of truth decided to reveal these mysteries for me, enabling me to see who He really is. He is the God who loves me enough to leave the comfort of Heaven, break into my world and die for me so I can have a personal relationship with Him, both now and forever more.

Another personal example of how truth can overcome the masks we have in our lives relate to when I became a staff member at the church I visited over thirty-three years ago. I happened to be there one morning a couple of years later, and a middle-aged man made an appointment to see me. This man was brilliant. He held two doctoral degrees in Chemistry. He had a prestigious job at a large, high-tech chemical company, and in our meeting he told me he had been searching for God, and truth, for a long time. Despite everything he had read and everyone he had talked to, nothing made sense. He had not found any satisfying answers to his questions. He explained he had come to our church the previous Sunday. This happened to be an unusual Sunday because the entire service had been geared towards children and their families.

God's ultimate plan is rapidly unfolding.

On this particular day, our children performed a play about the greatest story ever told. It was the story about God's plan to build an eternal family, and it was presented in a simple format that even a young child could comprehend. Now, this man, who held two PhDs and a prestigious scientific job, was there to watch. In spite of all the great theological works he had read about God and faith and eternity, none of them had ever made any sense. But on that pivotal Sunday as he watched a play with a simple message about God's grace, it became clear to him for the first time. The truth had finally been unveiled.

Mysteries are always being unveiled, and I believe that these seven foreshadows contain unique mysteries. These mysteries have been unveiled by the Holy Spirit for you and me, at a time such as this, when God's ultimate plan is rapidly unfolding. Now that we have our special "reading glasses" on, let's take a look at some ways we can learn about a few of God's most profound mysteries.

CHAPTER 2

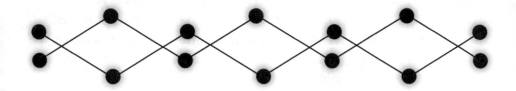

The Shadows of Things to Come

Answer the questions below. Think carefully about the answer to each one before reading further to see what the answers are.

1. Over a four-year calendar period, some months have thirty-one days, and others have thirty; how many months have twenty-eight days?

2. How many animals of each species did Moses take on the ark?

What was your answer to the first question? Most people respond by saying there is only one month that has twenty-eight days every fourth year, which is February. The correct answer? All of them do. Every month of every year has at least twenty-eight days.

How many animals of each species did Moses take on the ark?

Most people say two animals of each species were taken onto the ark. If this was your guess, you would be wrong. Why? Because Moses did not build the ark. Noah did. Do not feel silly if you were caught by this one—I made the same mistake when I was first asked this question. The person joked, "And you call yourself a pastor." Because the ark is mentioned, we focus on what we know, rather than what is being asked.

Incidentally, there is another reason you would be wrong. Noah needed animals to sacrifice for God. The text reads: "...seven of every kind of clean animal, a male and its mate, and two of every kind of unclean animal..." (Gen. 7:2).

The point I am trying to make is that many of us have difficulty solving word problems. I have struggled with them since childhood. My brain is not geared toward solving this sort of problem. It is sort of like the mask of Zorro mentioned in the previous chapter. Just as Zorro's mask kept everyone from recognizing Don Diego de la Vega, the truth is often mysteriously hidden, even though it is right in front of us.

DIVINE MYSTERIES

Did you know the Bible references specific phenomena it calls "divine mysteries?" It sounds kind of spooky, doesn't it?

A **divine mystery** is an event or a truth depicted in the Bible that is veiled or hidden from plain sight. A divine mystery cannot be understood until God chooses the appointed time to unveil this mystery. For example, Jesus spoke frequently to His disciples about how He was going to suffer and die, and how He would rise again on the third day. Yet in Luke's gospel, and in a few other places in scripture, we are made aware the disciples could not understand what Jesus was trying to say because it was hidden from them:

"Jesus took the Twelve aside and told them, 'We are

going up to Jerusalem, and everything that is written by the prophets about the Son of Man will be fulfilled. He will be handed over to the Gentiles. They will mock him, insult him, spit on him, flog him and kill him. On the third day he will rise again.' The disciples did not understand any of this. Its meaning was hidden from them, and they did not know what he was talking about" (Luke 18:31-34).

Why would Jesus take the time to tell His disciples something they could not understand? Most likely it is because Jesus knew the answers would be unveiled to them after He rose from the dead. John's gospel supports this speculation, when Jesus, speaking to His disciples, said, "I have much more to say to you, more than you can now bear. But when he, the Spirit of truth, comes, he will guide you into all truth..." (John 16:12-13).

Whatever reason Jesus had for telling His disciples things they could not understand, all the prophecies about the Messiah suffering were right there in the Hebrew Bible, in the first episode. But they were hidden from the eyes of the disciples until God chose the appropriate timing to unveil this truth to them.

The apostle Paul also referenced divine mysteries on numerous occasions, such as: Romans 16:26; Ephesians 3:9; and Colossians 1:26. These are just a few examples where Paul writes about divine mysteries, describing the fact that even though they have been kept hidden from ages past, these mysteries are now being unveiled to believers in the present age.

All the mysteries Paul refers to in these passages are events or truths in the Bible that remain veiled or hidden until God's appointed time. The events and truths to which he refers were very clearly written in the scriptures. Their exact meaning could not be understood until a specific time in history, which was appointed by God for their revelation. Stay with me—I'm building up to a concept I want you to grasp.

PROGRESSIVE FORESHADOWS

Let us consider a process through which God is unveiling what I call progressive foreshadows. A foreshadow is essentially one form of a divine mystery. A **foreshadow** is also categorized within the framework of biblical typology. Typology is the study of types and symbols. Typically, the term is associated with an allegory, in the sense it can be interpreted to unveil a hidden meaning. In the sense we will use it, typology refers to a picture from the Hebrew scriptures that is also intended to point to a future event or a future truth. The Book of Numbers, for example, tells the story of how the Israelites were grumbling in the wilderness, so God sent venomous snakes as a judgment (Num. 21:4-9). The people were being bitten by the snakes and dying. They realized they had sinned and asked for mercy. God then told Moses to make a bronze snake and put it up on a pole. Any Israelite who had been bitten could look up at the snake and live. Looking at the bronze serpent would save them from death.

A foreshadow is also categorized within the framework of biblical typology.

At face value, it really seems to be an odd event, especially when considered in isolation. Yet Jesus revealed this as a foreshadow: "Just as Moses lifted up the snake in the desert, so the Son of Man must be lifted up, that everyone who believes in him may have eternal life" (John 3:14-15).

Moses being instructed to raise up the bronze serpent on a pole enables us to recognize a type or picture that points us to how we can be saved from our sins if we simply "look up" to what Jesus accomplished for us when he hung on a cross (See Galatians 3:13).

It makes sense because why else would God take the time to send venomous snakes in the first place if all the Israelites had to do to be saved was to look up to a snake on a pole?

The moment we put on our special, Jewish-Christian reading glasses, it all makes perfect sense. Our special glasses enable us to comprehend God's deeper meaning behind this desperate situation. Recognizing the Israelites had to look up to the snake to be saved serves as a foreshadow of our desperate need to look up to Jesus so we, too, can be saved. And there are dozens of foreshadows like this one in our Bible. This series focuses on what I believe are the seven primary foreshadows that describe the Jewish people as a type. These seven foreshadows, when combined, create a powerful picture pointing to God's plan to build an eternal family.

I shared in the Introduction a little about how God had given me the content for this series. Now, let's back up just a little, so I can fill you in on what happened about two weeks prior. Just before God gave me the foreshadow series, I needed a new topic to preach on, and for the first time in my ministry I wasn't hearing from God. It was weird and very troubling for me personally. Until this point in my pastoral career, I had always felt a strong leading from the Holy Spirit concerning what I should preach. I had always felt confident when I showed up every Sunday to deliver my sermon. I consistently felt I had a God-inspired message to share, but for the first time, I felt no guide from the Spirit.

Out of desperation, I made a suggestion to the Cornerstone leadership team, saying, "Hey, why don't we do a series out of the book of Ephesians on who we are in Messiah?" Pretty cool, I thought... I mean, how could I go wrong preaching on a series of this nature?

"Yeah, that sounds pretty good," the leadership team agreed. "It should be a good series." The next day, my wife, Andrea, and I packed up and traveled to the mountains for a few days, where I could spend some quiet time working on this series. On the way up to Winter Park I started feeling sick, and by the time we arrived, I was struggling with severe symptoms of what appeared to be stomach flu. The next morning, I was horribly incapacitated, unable to study or prepare my series. I spent my time lying on the couch, or making frequent visits to the bathroom. Fortunately, I had planned for a guest speaker to preach that following Sunday, and by then I was feeling a little better, so I attended one of the services. I went up to the balcony so I would not infect anybody.

Now what I'm about to tell you is so surreal you might think I'm making it up, but members of the Cornerstone Congregation who were there know this story and can verify what happened. The guest speaker started his sermon by saying, "Most churches usually don't have any real focus or leading from the Holy Spirit, so they come up with just any idea that sounds good—like doing a series on who you are in Christ from the book of Ephesians."

I'm not kidding, it was almost what I suggested to the Cornerstone leadership verbatim. When I realized he was for real, and I wasn't having my leg pulled, I had no option but to consider what was unfolding, sensing it was for my benefit. As for the guest speaker, let's just say I didn't feel particularly friendly toward him at that point. *Who the heck do you think you are, coming into God's house...?*

That is funny, but the message felt like a direct slam from God. Thankfully, I had the grace to acknowledge it. *Alright Lord, you have my attention. You know I fell ill while trying to plan the series, now here You have a guy telling me I shouldn't do what I was planning to do... Alright. No series from the book of Ephesians on who we are in Christ. But what do You want me to do?*

It was that very evening I woke up around one in the morning, unable to sleep. I began reading my Bible, and something I found in the book of Colossians caught my attention:

> *"Therefore do not let anyone judge you by what you eat or drink, or with regard to a religious festival, a New Moon celebration or a Sabbath day. These are a shad-*

ow of the things that were to come; the reality, however,
is found in Christ" (Colossians 2:16-17).

I stopped on the part that said the reality of these shadows are found in the Messiah. I was intrigued. What further caught my attention is this passage mentions the annual Jewish feasts, the New Moon celebrations, and the weekly Sabbaths, explaining that these events are shadows of some future reality. As I read this passage in the early hours of the morning, I began to wonder if the Bible mentions any other shadows in a similar manner. A quick word search revealed two more references to the word, "shadow."

First I saw the book of Hebrews tells us the Earthly temple "... is a copy and shadow of what is in heaven..." (Heb. 8:5), and we know from other scriptures this Heavenly temple will one day be established on Earth. The second reference I found was also from Hebrews, and it said the Torah—or Law—is also "...only a shadow..." of a future reality (Heb. 10:1).

For the next four days I averaged about two hours of sleep per night, completely absorbed in studying this topic. The interesting thing is that at no point during this time did I feel tired. I had never felt more energized in my life. It was strange, but exhilarating at the same time. I felt as though I had experienced a divinely appointed spiritual event, almost frenzied in its intensity. I had never experienced anything quite like it, neither prior to that week, nor ever since that time.

What I discovered was entirely fascinating—the common link between all these foreshadows. Together, they create a comprehensive picture of Abraham's Earthly family—the Jewish people, the Israelites. Abraham's Earthly family in turn, is a foreshadow of God's plan to establish an eternal family. By the end of the week, God had shown me there were seven foreshadows in all, which is not surprising, as seven is the biblical number of perfection.

The Seven Foreshadows are as follows:

1. **THE COVENANT**, which is God's irrevocable promises given to Abraham in a form resembling the life-long commitment for in a marriage.

2. A marriage is usually followed by children, which pertains to the **NATION OF ISRAEL**, the family.

3. When you have a family it's necessary to have a place to live, and this is why God gave Israel **THE PROMISED LAND**—their family home.

4. To ensure the health of a family, it needs a set of rules to live by, which is why God gave Israel **THE TORAH**, the family rules.

5. In a healthy family, everyone has safe and easy access to Dad, which comes through **THE TEMPLE** foreshadow.

6. **THE SABBATH** provides one day each week to cease from their work.

7. **THE FEASTS** provide annual family gatherings that build up to a triumphant harvest celebration.

Notice how well these foreshadows fit and flow together. Linking these seven foreshadows creates a beautiful picture of an ethnic family—a family God would establish through the lineage of a man named Abraham. Together, these linked events create a shadow, or a *type*, intended to lead us to the eternal family God is establishing through faith in the Mashiach—the Messiah.

Each foreshadow operates effectively on its own merit to deliver a powerful message. The real power, however, is to see how God knits these seven foreshadows together to form one beautiful and brilliant foreshadow story.

THE SEVEN FORESHADOWS POINT US TO GOD'S GOAL TO ESTABLISH OF AN ETERNAL FAMILY

To fully grasp what a shadow is, let's consider how we perceive a **shadow** and what this means. When the sun shines onto an object, the object casts what we call a shadow onto the surface beyond itself. While the shadow is connected to the real object, and resembles the shape of it, we are clearly able to recognize the shadow is not the actual object. If we were in a building and you saw lights shining onto me, you would certainly be able to see my shadow. When you look at my shadow, you would never say, "Hey, there's Gene." The more appropriate response would be to point out, "There's Gene's shadow." If you only saw my shadow, and you wanted to find me, you would follow my shadow until you could see where it met my body, at which point you could confidently say, "Oh, there he is."

Similarly, the purpose of these seven foreshadows is to lead us to the real thing. This is why Paul states clearly in his epistle to the Galatians, "...the law (Torah) was put in charge to *lead us to Christ* (Messiah) that we might be justified by faith" (Gal. 3:24). The same principle applies to the Law, as referenced in Hebrews: "The law is only a shadow of the good things that are coming— not the realities themselves" (Heb. 10:1).

The point to be made is, all seven foreshadows, representing a comprehensive picture of Abraham's family, are meant to lead us toward God's ultimate goal of establishing an eternal family. One remarkable aspect of these foreshadows is they all unfold in the same systematic, three-episode, progressive pattern that reflects the tri-episodic nature of God, as described in the scriptures. Episode one consists of the prophetic pictures of the God who was in the past; episode two incorporates the Messianic fulfillments of the God who is in the present; and episode three holds the eternal completions of the God who will be in the future. The Torah is a good example of how a foreshadow unfolds in these three-episode progressions.

The fourth foreshadow deals specifically with the Torah but let's have a quick sneak preview of what Jesus had to say in Matthew's gospel: "Do not think that I have come to abolish the Law or the Prophets; I have not come to abolish them but to fulfill them" (Matt. 5:17). Notice how Jesus says, "I have not come to abolish" the Law or the Prophets, "but to fulfill them." This is a place you can see Jesus inferring we're moving from episode one to episode two. Jesus gave this explanation to show us how the Torah was a shadow in episode one, intended to lead us to Him. At the same time, when Jesus said He was here not to abolish the Torah but to fulfill it, He was also welcoming us to episode two. This will become more clear when we look at the Torah foreshadow later on.

Jesus then goes on to say, "I tell you the truth, until heaven and earth disappear, not the smallest letter, not the least stroke of a pen, will by any means disappear from the Law until everything is accomplished" (Matt. 5:18). Notice how Jesus says, "...until heaven and earth disappear," at the beginning of the verse, and how He ends the verse by saying, "...until everything is accomplished." Jesus does this to bring our attention to the third and final episode of the Torah foreshadow in God's great trilogy. The final episode will take place in the future, with the new Heaven and new Earth spoken of in Isaiah 65:17 and Revelation 21:1–2.

At this point in God's story, when all these astonishing foreshadows that represent a comprehensive picture of Israel, are brought to their eternal completion, we ride off into the sunset with our great Hero, to live happily ever after.

For me, what is amazing is recognizing how all seven foreshadows unfold in this same systematic, three-episode progression. Likewise, when you see how these foreshadows unfold, I believe it will build your faith immeasurably, taking it to an unprecedented level.

Recognizing how these foreshadows unfold will also help you see how God is unquestionably in control of history, even when it looks like things are chaotic from our perspective. Furthermore, this knowledge will help you see how God is directing your life. He is the Author of your story. God wrote the trilogy. He also wrote your story, and both of them will conclude exactly the way He wrote it.

But before we delve into this, I want to make sure we all have 20/20 vision as we study these foreshadows. There is just one more thing we need to address. You may not even be aware of this elephant in the room, as it sits here, trumpeting and waving its trunk around. I am talking about something called *Replacement Theology*. Replacement Theology seeks to nullify the promises God made to Abraham and his descendants, and the scary thing is, it is taught in many churches around the world today. I want to ensure that you do not somehow reach the conclusion that these foreshadows rescind God's promises to the Jewish people in any way. Let's take a look.

CHAPTER 3

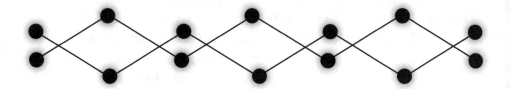

Replacement Theology

B efore we explore the seven foreshadows, it is important to first expose a false and dangerous teaching, called Replacement Theology. Many Christians have never heard of this term, but it's deeply embedded into the DNA of many churches today. I believe that no single doctrine has taken the Church farther off course than Replacement Theology.

Replacement Theology, also known as *supersessionism* or *fulfillment theology*, began to surface in the Church as early as the end of the first century A.D. According to this errant doctrine, because the Jewish people rejected Jesus as the Messiah and had Him executed, God subsequently rejected the Jewish people. Many took it even further, saying God now despises the Jewish people. They believe that as a result of the Jewish people's actions, God consequently revoked the literal promises He made to Abraham and his family and replaced them with spiritual promises to the Church. This is replacement theology in short summation. In other words, the Church supersedes Israel, hence the term, *supersessionism.*

This heretical teaching has unfortunately led to an extreme anti-Jewish attitude throughout most of Christianity's history, by the very Church whose roots are Jewish. This anti-Jewish attitude resulted in countless Jews being persecuted and even murdered in the name of Jesus, if you can imagine that. The Crusades, the Inquisition, and the Holocaust are three of the most well-known of these events. There have been, however, innumerable acts of hatred toward the Jewish people throughout Christianity's 2000-year history that were directly influenced by Replacement Theology.

No single doctrine has taken the Church farther off course than Replacement Theology.

If you find that difficult to believe, consider that many of our Church fathers including Ignatius, Irenaeus, Tertullian, Justin Martyr, Origen, Chrysostom, St. Augustine, and even Martin Luther held very anti-Jewish views. These views were largely because of being blinded by the doctrine of Replacement Theology. These revered churchmen often spoke and wrote adversely about the Jews and referred to them using derogatory terms, such as "pigs" or "dogs." These leader held to the belief Jewish people were not worthy of God's salvation because they rejected and murdered His son. Here are just a few quotes from their teaching:

"Jews are disinherited from the grace of God." (Irenaeus Bishop of Lyon AD 177)

"God has rejected the Jews in favor of the Christians."

(Tertullian, circa AD 200)

"The Jews are the most worthless of all men. They are lecherous, rapacious, greedy. They are perfidious murderers of Christ. They worship the Devil. Their religion is a sickness. The Jews are the odious assassins of Christ and for killing God there is no expiation possible, no indulgence or pardon. Christians may never cease vengeance, and the Jew must live in servitude forever. God always hated the Jews. It is essential that all Christians hate them." (Oration against the Jews, John Chrysostom 349 CE-407 CE)[2]

Martin Luther, considered to be the father of Protestantism, was a powerful force in reforming the Church. Initially, Luther fought against the widespread anti-Jewish attitude within the Church, but later in life spoke out forcefully against the Jews when they rejected the Gospel. In 1543 Luther wrote a book titled, *On the Jews and their Lies*, which is still available today. Luther advocates burning down all the synagogues in Europe, as well as expelling all the Jews from Europe. Adolph Hitler's hatred of the Jewish people was partly inspired by Luther's anti-Jewish teachings and Hitler often referred to Luther as one of Germany's great reformers.[3]

This flawed teaching unfortunately lingers in various forms in many churches today. It may be subtle, but it's still prevalent, and it influences the attitude many Christians have toward Jewish people and their practices. One easily identifiable example of this attitude that is most relevant to this book is the view that Jewish people no longer have a viable role to play in God's story. This attitude suggests there is no longer any place for ethnic Israel to

2 Hitler, Adolf. (1971). Mein kampf. Boston & New York: Houghton Mifflin Company.
3 Wiener, Peter F. (1999). Martin Luther: Hitler's spiritual ancestor. Cranford, New Jersey: American Atheist Press.

live in the Land of Israel—at least not in the prophetic sense of returning from their long, 2000-year exile to the Promised Land. Proponents of this view today believe the Jewish people no longer have any claim to the Land and are merely intruders and occupiers in the Land.

REPLACEMENT THEOLOGY AND THE MODERN CHURCH

Here is an examination of how Replacement Theology has influenced the thinking of modern Christians:

First and foremost, most Christians today are not anti-Jewish, they are just misinformed. Many are taught incorrectly that the Church has replaced Israel, and there is no longer any actual role for ethnic Israel in God's story. This often leads Christians to develop an unfavorable view of the Jewish people, especially toward Jews living in the Land of Israel. This view also contributes to an unbalanced belief that the Palestinian Arabs are exclusively the good guys while the Israeli Jews are exclusively the bad guys.

Second, on the other end of the spectrum, are Christians who are correctly taught from the scripture that it is God's prophetic plan for the Jewish people to return to the Land. This leads these Christians to have a favorable view of the Jewish people, but can also contribute to an unbalanced belief that the Israeli Jews are the good guys while the Palestinian Arabs are the bad guys. Some in this camp incorrectly teach that all Palestinians do not want peace and will only be satisfied to see the Jewish people destroyed. While it is true that there are some voices calling for the destruction of the Jewish people, most Palestinians and Jews want to find a peaceful solution to their longstanding conflict.

I spend a lot of time traveling between America and Israel. I know firsthand how complicated the Israeli-Palestinian conflict is. And it will likely continue to be complicated until the Messiah establishes His eternal Kingdom at the end of God's story. The moment anyone thinks they have a simple solution to this complex problem, they have essentially become part of the problem. Even so, it is important never to lose sight of one simple fact: every human on this planet is made in the image and likeness of God. Every single person. This means everyone deserves to be treated with dignity and respect. There can be no deviation to this rule. This is perhaps the best sentiment for both sides to bear in mind when we think about the Israeli-Palestinian conflict.

Some are more concerned about Israel's right to exist safely in the Land as a sovereign state, while others are more concerned about Palestinians living in poor conditions. Remember, that not everyone in God's plan is acting within His perfect will. There are sinners on the Israeli side not doing God's will, and there are sinners on the Palestinian side not doing God's will. This has led to the problems both ethnic groups face. God, however, still has a plan, and all are invited—even urged—to be part of His Kingdom (Matt. 28:16-20).

I share this information because as we begin to explore the seven foreshadows, you will start to realize how the Jewish people are a shadow of the real thing to come. It is therefore critical for us to understand the key role they play, and will continue to play, in God's story throughout all three episodes.

SPIRITUAL ISRAEL VERSUS ETHNIC ISRAEL

Most people whom have been influenced by Replacement Theology today believe there is no longer any role for ethnic Israel in God's story and view the Church as the true spiritual Israel. According to them, ethnic Israel lost its claim to God's physical promises through unbelief; and spiritual Israel, the elect—the Church—has always been the intended recipients of God's promises. To them, God's physical promises to ethnic Israel were dependent on Israel's faithfulness, not God's, and they were just a foreshadow to the real spiritual promises He actually meant to give to the elect. If this teaching seems to be inconsistent with a God who keeps His promises and does not engage in bait and switch tactics, it may now become clear why I am dedicating an entire chapter to this subject.

On the other hand, those who see the error of Replacement Theology, clearly understand there is a continued role for ethnic Israel throughout God's story. This is because they know God is a promise keeper and He will keep the promises He made to Abraham's family. Many in this camp have contempt for the term "spiritual Israel" even though it is taught in the scriptures. This is because to them any teaching of a spiritual Israel implies God's physical promises to ethnic Israel have been nullified.

As with some seemingly paradoxical doctrines like freewill, predestination, eternal security, and apostasy, both sides usually ignore each other's scriptural arguments. The truth lies somewhere in the middle. To explain further, understand that spiritual Israel—the elect—are spoken of clearly and are patterned after Abraham, who believed the Lord in faith, and it was credited "... to him as righteousness" (Gen. 15:6). So, as the New Testament scriptures state, those who have faith, are then the children of Abraham: "If you belong to Christ (Messiah), then you are Abraham's seed, and heirs according to the promise" (Gal. 3:29). This concept is clarified in Paul's letter to the Roman Church:

> *"It is not as though God's word had failed. For not all who are descended from Israel are Israel. Nor because they are his descendants are they all Abraham's children. On the contrary, 'It is through Isaac that your offspring will be reckoned.' In other words, it is not the natural children who are God's children, but it is the children of the promise who are regarded as Abraham's offspring" (Romans 9:6-8).*

In every generation, God always had a righteous remnant or a group of true believers who believed God and lived by faith, not by works, but because of the work God did for us on the cross. This is known as spiritual Israel, and it is distinctly taught in the Bible.

The Bible also clearly teaches that God will fulfill his covenant promises to ethnic Israel, not because of their works, but because of God's faithfulness. Yes, there were disciplinary consequences for Israel's unfaithfulness, and so on two occasions, God exiled them from the Promised Land. However, each time God had a plan to bring them back. There is no controversy that God intended to bring the Jewish people back from Babylon during the first exile. The books of Nehemiah and Ezra go into great detail about it. This was a regional exile that only lasted seventy years. God also had a plan to return the Jewish people to the Promised Land a second time, however this time it will be from a global exile that ended up lasting 2,000 years. The Romans expelled the Jews from Israel in AD 70 and this time they were scattered to the four corners of the world. Isaiah clearly spoke about Israel's return to the land from this second exile:

> *"In that day the Lord will reach out his hand a second time to reclaim the remnant that is left of his people from Assyria, from Lower Egypt, from Upper Egypt, from Cush, from Elam, from Babylonia, from Hamath and from the islands of the sea. He will raise a banner for the nations and gather the exiles of Israel; he will assemble the scattered people of Judah from the four quarters of the earth"* (Isa. 11:11-12).

In addition, most of the Jewish prophets go into great detail about the turbulent events that will take place at the end of God's story—the last days. Most of those events take place in Israel and it is evident from these passages that Israel is inhabited by Jews during that time. Even Jesus presumes Jews will be living in Israel when he talks about those troubling events in Matthew 24. What you cannot find is a verse in scripture that claims God abandoned His covenant promises with Israel. The opposite is true, as is exemplified in Romans:

> *"And so all Israel will be saved, as it is written: 'The deliverer will come from Zion; he will turn godlessness away from Jacob. And this is my covenant with them when I take away their sins.' As far as the gospel is concerned, they are enemies on your account; but as far as election is concerned, they are loved on account of the patriarchs, for God's gifts and his call are irrevocable"* (Rom. 11:26-29).

Here in the letter to the church in Rome, Paul reinforces God's faithfulness in keeping His covenant promises to Abraham and his family. When we look at the first foreshadow, which is The Covenant, it will become remarkably clear this covenant was an unbreakable promise made by God to Israel. Because of their unfaithfulness, God exiled the Jews from their homeland twice in their history but He will ultimately keep His promise, "...for God's gifts and his call are irrevocable." Every promise God made to Israel is guaranteed through God's faithfulness to His people, not through their faithfulness to Him.

Consider for a moment what Replacement Theology is actually suggesting. If God can break the promises He made to the Jewish people, what hope do we have that God will keep the promises He has made to His Church? For this reason we should desperately hope God will honor His promises to Israel. Thankfully, God truly is a promise keeper. If we put on our Jewish-Christian glasses, we will see how God indeed keeps every promise He has ever made throughout history, whether to Israel or the Church.

Scripture goes so far as to explicitly proclaim, "...it is impossible for God to lie..." (Heb. 6:18). Yet God never once promised His story would not take twists and turns, with us experiencing some nail-biting events until all His promises are fulfilled. And yes, we are currently in an extremely anxiety-filled and "nail-biting" period of the story.

Another aspect of God's story is the specific role Israel has played, especially regarding their persecution throughout history. When God chose the Jewish people to play this important role in His story, it is almost as if they were marked with a bulls' eye on their backs. Recognizing their role, Satan has tried everything he can to remove the Jewish people from the story. Satan is so cunning, as we saw, he has even used the Church to help vilify the Jews. Yet the Jewish people continue to play a key role in God's story, and make no mistake, it's a tough role to play. Reading through Jewish history reveals what a difficult history theirs has been.

God did not choose the Jewish people because they were a large nation or were more powerful than any other nation. God purposely chose them for qualities that oppose those things to show off His name. God made this clear, speaking through the prophet, Ezekiel:

> *"Therefore say to the house of Israel, 'This is what the Sovereign LORD says: It is not for your sake, O house of Israel, that I am going to do these things [in the context of fulfilling His covenant promises], but for the sake of my holy name, which you have profaned among the nations where you have gone'" (Ezek. 36:22).*

God chose an insignificant, weak, rebellious, and unfaithful people so He could show off His name to the world. He has chosen us for the same reason (1 Cor. 1:27-29). When we personalize this idea it makes more sense. We are all insignificant, weak, rebellious, and unfaithful, and God did not choose any of us for our own sake. He chose us for His holy name, for His name's sake, for His glory.

Why would God do this? Because He wants to show the world that it is all about *His* faithfulness and not ours. How many people are truly faithful all the time? None. But God *is* faithful. He also wants to show the world that it is all about His power, not ours. It is ultimately about His story and not ours. We might think we are something of special importance, but the only One who is a Hero in this story is God. He alone is God, and there is none like Him.

The premise of this book is that ethnic Israel is a foreshadow of God's plan to build an eternal family. Do not confuse this beautiful foreshadowing of the Jewish people with the destructive foreshadowing of Replacement Theology. Do not think for a single second this material suggests the Church has replaced Israel in any way. Satan would like nothing more than to make evil out of something God intended for good. After 2,000 years of exile, the Jews are back in the Promised Land. It's still a messy story with lots of nail-biting twists and turns, but God is a promise keeper, and one day He will fulfill all his promises to Israel, as He will to the Church—probably at the same time. At that time, there will be no more conflict, no more nail-biting twists and turns. There will only be everlasting *shalom* as the nations live together forever in perfect harmony in the place the

Why would God do this?

In closing, Apostle Paul, as he was inspired by the Holy Spirit, spoke on the main subject of this chapter:

> *"I do not want you to be ignorant of this mystery, brothers, so that you may not be conceited: Israel has experienced a hardening in part until the full number of the Gentiles has come in. And so all Israel will be saved, as it is written: 'The deliverer will come from*

Zion; he will turn godlessness away from Jacob. And this is my covenant with them when I take away their sins.' As far as the gospel is concerned, they are enemies on your account; but as far as election is concerned, they are loved on account of the patriarchs, for God's gifts and his call are irrevocable. Just as you who were at one time disobedient to God have now received mercy as a result of their disobedience, so they too have now become disobedient in order that they too may now receive mercy as a result of God's mercy to you. For God has bound all men over to disobedience so that he may have mercy on them all. Oh, the depth of the riches of the wisdom and knowledge of God! How unsearchable his judgments, and his paths beyond tracing out! Who has known the mind of the Lord? Or who has been his counselor? Who has ever given to God, that God should repay him?' For from him and through him and to him are all things. To him be the glory forever! Amen" (Rom. 11:25-36).

That was certainly a lot of information to consider, but we can now go forward without hesitation, especially concerning God's blueprint for His Church. Given this solid foundation, let's take a look at our first foreshadow, The Covenant.

PART II

CHAPTER 4

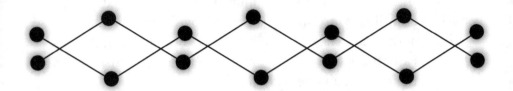

The Covenant, Episode No. 1: The Engagement Gone Badly

"...until death do us part"

There is nothing more devastating to a relationship than unfaithfulness. Some say the death of a loved one is less difficult to grieve than the unfaithfulness of a spouse. The book of Hosea is written to help us understand how heart-broken God feels when we are unfaithful to Him. It is also an explicit indication of how God's faithfulness to us is not dependent on our faithfulness to Him. As we will see in detail in this chapter, the prophet Hosea documented his personal love story reflecting the chronic unfaithfulness he experienced in his own marriage. The fascinating part about his story is it captures in heart-wrenching detail the destruction unfaithfulness brings and how this parallels our relationship with God.

We all know that when a bride and bridegroom declare their wedding vows to one another, they are making a solemn vow to remain faithful to each other through any trial or tribulation they may face until they are finally separated by death. Yet well over half of modern marriages fail to keep this vow. How can this be? Humans are sinful, flawed, and imperfect beings. Because of this, we experience difficulty being faithful.

As we study this first foreshadow—"The Covenant"—it is important for us to recognize that in contrast to our modern mind-set, God always keeps His promises. He has a 100-percent perfect record of faithfulness throughout history. God understands how our sinfulness corrupts our attempts at faithfulness. Time and time again, no matter how we strive to be faithful, we continually fall short of this goal, but God still remains true to us. This, of course, does not make it okay for us to sin. To the contrary, it is in spite of our serial infidelity that God is faithful to us. What's more is unlike our human vows, not even our death will affect God's faithfulness to us. He promises are *eternal*.

Having established this essential aspect of God's nature, I would like to share another personal love story with you.

A HIPPIE LOVE STORY

Once upon a time, in the early Seventies, there was a remarkably handsome Jewish hippie named Gene, and an extraordinarily cute Gentile flower child named Andrea. Gene and Andrea met one day, fell in love, and began dating. They had lots of fun together, tripping out in the park, and saying things like, "far out" and "groovy." Soon after, the hippie and flower child decided to get married. They had a traditional Jewish wedding, pledged their covenant vows to each other under the *chuppah*, and smashed cake into each other's faces—signifying their deep love for one another. They then headed off in their matching denim leisure suits to live happily ever after. Yes, this is a description of how I met and married my beautiful wife. But the leisure suits should have been a huge red flag, as trouble loomed around the next corner.

The hippie and flower child soon had two beautiful babies, Lisa and Michael. This happy little family created a myriad of groovy family memories like camping and road trips to far-out places. After a few blissful years of marriage, ominous clouds gathered on the horizon. The once-happy hippie and the formerly footloose flower child experienced major marital turbulence. In the seventh year of marriage, the unthinkable happened: unfaithfulness entered the marriage relationship, and the woeful couple separated.

It was a dark, sad time, leaving both feeling distraught and miserable. The broken family tried to cope with the consequences of their shattered hopes and dreams, and stifle the pain of broken vows. Separation is never easy, but for a married couple with children, the heartache is excruciating. Yet, God would not give up on His original plan for their lives. A wild and mystifying miracle occurred and the hippie and flower child reunited. Even more astonishing was that they both found their Mashiach. The one and only Son of God, Yeshua. He healed their pain, suffering, and confusion. As the family began to experience a new and better freedom, their loving and faithful God totally healed and restored their marriage. At the time of this book being written, the hippie and the flower child have been married for over forty-three years. God makes everything groovy.

Given this wild and mystifying miracle, this heartache turned groovy by God, I could easily have titled this chapter, "Wild Thing." I just had to put it out there though, for fellow hippies who will appreciate how a person's heart can sing again. Especially when embraced by the true God of love and peace who created all the flowers and everything else we find so wonderful.

THE COVENANT IN THREE EPISODES

Ironically, our story has parallels similar to those reflected in the story of God and the Israelites. God's relationship with the Jewish people, The Covenant, is the literal foundation upon which all the other foreshadows are established. All foreshadows follow this form, and like all the others, The Covenant foreshadow will unfold over three captivating episodes throughout the course of history.

Episode one is the past-prophetic picture of God's betrothal to Israel—an engagement in which Israel becomes unfaithful. Episode two is the present-Messianic fulfillment that heralds the reconciliation of this marriage. And episode three is the future-eternal completion of the wedding in an idyllic paradise called New Jerusalem.

The Covenant foreshadow will unfold over three captivating episodes throughout the course of history.

Let's take a closer look at this very special love story called "The Covenant" by first recognizing it as a prophetic picture of an engagement that results in one party being unfaithful. Several generations into God's wild story, He appeared to an old, childless, (and probably toothless) man named Abram. God promised Abram that even though he and his wife, Sarai, are childless and homeless, they will have descendants as numerous as the stars of the sky, and they will be given a homeland flowing with milk and honey. Because this all happened in the past, we know this couple's descendants are called "Israelites," and the homeland they received is known as "Israel."

God first promised Abram (who would later become Abraham)

that He would bless him with innumerable descendants, saying:

> *"Lift up your eyes from where you are and look north and south, east and west. All the land that you see I will give to you and your offspring forever. I will make your offspring like the dust of the earth, so that if anyone could count the dust, then your offspring could be counted. Go, walk through the length and breadth of the land, for I am giving it to you" (Gen. 13:14-17).*

Later, after Lot had parted from his uncle, God again promised Abram he would father many children and be given a great land: "...'Look up at the heavens and count the stars—if indeed you can count them.' Then he said to him, 'So shall your offspring be'" (Gen. 15:5). He also said to him, '...I am the LORD, who brought you out of Ur of the Chaldeans to give you this land to take possession of it'" (Gen. 15:7).

Again in Genesis 17:1-8, we see God even increase His promises when He makes this powerful and symbolic covenant with Abram. He even renamed him from Abram which means "exalted father," to "Abraham," meaning, "father of many":

> *"When Abram was ninety-nine years old, the LORD appeared to him and said, 'I am God Almighty; walk before me and be blameless. I will confirm my covenant between me and you and will greatly increase your numbers.' Abram fell facedown, and God said to him, 'As for me, this is my covenant with you: You will be the father of many nations. No longer will you be called Abram; your name will be Abraham, for I have made you a father of many nations. I will make you very fruitful; I will make nations of you, and kings will come from you. I will establish my covenant as an everlasting covenant between me and you and your*

descendants after you for the generations to come, to be your God and the God of your descendants after you. The whole land of Canaan, where you are now an alien, I will give as an everlasting possession to you and your descendants after you; and I will be their God."

This scripture is significant. God mentions one crucial word that would bind Him to this promise for eternity: notice the word *everlasting* in verse seven above. The Covenant that God makes with Abraham is everlasting, which means God will remain faithful to His word forever, *even when the Israelites become unfaithful to Him.* That is powerful.

After this, when Abraham was ninety-nine years old, he was visited by the Lord who decided it was time to bring His promise into the immediate future. He told Abraham that his wife, Sarah, would bear him a son. But being well past childbearing age, Sarah laughed to herself. God told Abraham He would return the same time the following year and his wife would have a son (See Genesis 18:10). True to God's word, Sarah bore Abraham a son "...at the very time God had promised him" (See Genesis 21:2). Abraham named the promised child Isaac, who was born when Abraham was a hundred years old and Sarah was ninety-nine. From this single child, the new nation of Israel emerged, and they would eventually settle in the Promised Land.

The interesting thing to note is how the Covenant promises God made to Abraham and his descendants are intended to parallel the ancient covenant promises Jewish couples made to each other in their marriage ritual. Throughout the Bible, and especially in the books of the prophets, God uses terminology that typifies language a husband would use when speaking to his wife. We find one direct example in Isaiah when God says to the nation of Israel, "For your Maker is your husband—the LORD Almighty is his name..." (Isa. 54:5). We also find another direct example in Jeremiah 31:31-32:

> " 'The time is coming,' declares the LORD, 'when I will
> make a new covenant with the house of Israel and with
> the house of Judah. It will not be like the covenant I
> made with their forefathers when I took them by the
> hand to lead them out of Egypt, because they broke my
> covenant, though I was a husband to them,' declares
> the LORD."

OTHER EXAMPLES OF GOD USING MARITAL LANGUAGE IN THE SCRIPTURES

In another example, the prophet, Ezekiel, also writes about God's intimate relationship with Israel and the language God uses to describe His relationship with Israel is flirtatious, if not positively seductive:

> *"Later I passed by, and when I looked at you and saw
> that you were old enough for love, I spread the corner
> of my garment over you and covered your nakedness. I
> gave you my solemn oath and entered into a covenant
> with you, declares the Sovereign LORD, and you be-
> came mine" (Ezek. 16:8).*

I think it is safe to assume God is interested in being more than just friends with Israel.

God clearly had a marriage and a family in mind when He made this covenant with Abraham. The Abrahamic covenant is just the engagement or the betrothal phase of this relationship. The actual marriage won't take place until the distant future. It occurs in the third and final episode of God's wonderful story. Another important aspect of ancient Jewish law to note is that being engaged was as legally binding as being married. According to ancient Jewish law, if you wanted to break off an engagement you had to obtain a certificate of divorce to do so.

Let's consider the example of Joseph and Mary as explained in the Gospel of Matthew:

> "This is how the birth of Jesus Christ came about: His mother Mary was pledged to be married to Joseph, but before they came together, she was found to be with child through the Holy Spirit. Because Joseph her husband was a righteous man and did not want to expose her to public disgrace, he had in mind to divorce her quietly" (Matthew 1:18-19).

When we look at how the birth of Messiah Yeshua came about, we see that His mother, Mary, was pledged—meaning betrothed or engaged to be married—to Joseph. But before they came together—meaning they had not yet consummated their union through sexual relations—Mary was found to be with child through the Holy Spirit.

At this point they were bindingly betrothed to each other. They had signed a *ketubah*, which is a covenant promise similar in some ways to a modern prenuptial agreement. However, sometime after making their promises to each other, a little baby bump arose in their relationship. Mary had become pregnant, and Joseph knew he was not the father. Mary had been supernaturally impregnated through the power of the Holy Spirit, yet the credibility of Mary's claim is, understandably, too difficult for Joseph to bear. How many men wouldn't feel the same way? We discover in verse nineteen that although Joseph is a very good man, he is also a hurt man. The pain he felt over what he initially considered to be Mary's betrayal drove his decision to quietly divorce her. He chose this route to avoid publicly embarrassing Mary. Notice that Joseph is referred to as Mary's "husband," even though they are only engaged. Notice also how Joseph would have to divorce Mary to terminate their relationship, even though they were only engaged at this point.

We can see that Joseph and Mary's relationship started off on rocky ground before they were even married. But then again, so did God's relationship with Israel. God made a marital pledge to Israel but before the pledge was fulfilled, Israel became unfaithful to God, and fooled around with a host of other lovers. The Bible identifies these other lovers as "idols." An idol is anything that turns us away from God or removes us from His presence. Most people have no idea how Israel's adulterous relationship with these other lovers shattered God's heart. Israel's callous approach to her betrothal covenant came as a crushing blow to her Husband, who was God. Before the wedding invitations could even be mailed out, it seemed the marriage would be called off.

As we know, God is a promise-keeper. Because it is impossible for God to lie, He never breaks His promises. Obviously disappointed but willing to reconcile His betrothed to Him through marriage, God unveiled His courageous plan of reconciliation. This magnificent plan would take place in episode two of God's trilogy, which is incidentally that nail-biting part of the story in which you and I are currently involved.

> Obviously disappointed but willing to reconcile His betrothed to Him through marriage, God unveiled His courageous plan of reconciliation.

Now one thing I know is we *all* play a role in this great story written by God. Every single one of us. Whether you realize it or not, you play a role. Some of us, though, are chosen to have more difficult roles than others. Take Judas, for example. Imagine being the disciple who betrayed Jesus. Speaking to His disciples about Judas, Jesus stated, "...None has been lost except the one doomed to destruction so that Scripture would be fulfilled" (John 17:12). Considering Judas' betrayal, subsequent guilt, and suicide, it's a role in God's story I personally would prefer not to play.

I'd much rather play King David's role, bravely slaying the Philistine giant, Goliath. Or perhaps Joshua's role, marching around the walls of Jericho seven times until they collapsed. I think another rewarding role would be the Balaam's talking donkey. It is just a cameo appearance, but how incredible to play the part of just a talking donkey, rather than Judas.

Consider another extremely difficult role in God's story—one of our aforementioned prophets, Hosea, took on a seriously tough job. God immortalizes Hosea's story to show us how He feels about our unfaithfulness to Him. God told this good Jewish boy to go out and marry a wife who would completely wreck his life for a time. His wife, Gomer, would cheat on him not just once, but at least twice. We don't really know how many times she cheated on him (Hosea 1:2). Not everyone agrees, but the text seems to imply, as many scholars believe, that Hosea's children were conceived by other men. Imagine what it must have been like in Hosea's role. Imagine the heartache and anguish experienced by this young Jewish man, whose hopes and dreams for the future surely never included anything so gut-wrenching. This role just does not appeal to our human nature in any way. Nobody would ever desire to have this scenario unfold as part of their story. Yet, because of us, God experiences this torment every day.

Of course, God had a purpose for Hosea's story. He wanted to demonstrate to us on a human level how He feels when we cheat on Him. In chapter two, God begins to express how tortured He is by Israel's betrayal. We are given a detailed picture of God's heart-felt pain and anger as He vents over Israel's adultery. At the start of chapter two it seems the marriage will be called off. We cannot help feeling God's agony:

> *"Rebuke your mother, rebuke her, for she is not my wife, and I am not her husband. Let her remove the adulterous look from her face and the unfaithfulness from between her breasts" (Hosea 2:2).*

These raw emotions continue to be expressed for another eleven verses.

After God has spoken His mind on the matter, His true character shows. The Lord's anger starts to dissipate, and His language becomes soft again. He is still deeply in love with His betrothed. Next, something remarkable happens. In verse fourteen, the Lord talks about a day in the distant future, when He will again lure His beloved back into His arms.

Having vented, God makes this courageous statement of reconciliation:

> *"I will betroth you to me forever; I will betroth you in righteousness and justice, in love and compassion. I will betroth you in faithfulness, and you will acknowledge the LORD" (Hosea 2:19-20).*

Yet again, God uses language to illustrate His eternal connection with His chosen bride, His beloved. He says, "forever." Much like the "everlasting" covenant foreshadowed with Abraham and his descendants, He makes it clear Israel's sin cannot and will not be allowed to separate her from His love. This is a theme recognized by Paul when writing his epistle to the Romans in our current, second episode:

"For I am convinced that neither death nor life, neither angels nor demons, neither the present nor the future, nor any powers, neither height nor depth, nor anything else in all creation, will be able to separate us from the love of God that is in Christ (Messiah) Jesus our Lord" (Rom. 8:38-39).

Did you see that? *Nothing* can separate us from God's unconditional love. What a mind-blowing revelation.

That was quite a ride now, wasn't it? What a glorious God of promise. Now we have the foundation to grasp the next development in God's beautiful story. The next chapter will explore how God deals with the process of reconciliation in episode two of the Covenant foreshadow, and how He ensured His marriage would not become a byte of divorce data like so many in our sad human statistic.

CHAPTER 5

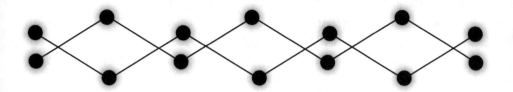

Covenant, Episode No. 2: The Reconciliation of the Marriage

"May the Lord deal with me, be it ever so severely, if anything but death separates you and me."
—Ruth 1:17

Toward the close of the last chapter, we saw God's raw, heart-wrenching emotions being expressed in the second chapter of Hosea. Venting His frustration at an unfaithful partner, God processed His anger, then reminded Himself (and Hosea) that He is an eternally faithful God. Even though Israel had been unfaithful to Him, He would never be unfaithful to Israel. Although God will go on to discipline Israel severely for her unfaithfulness, at this point, He is looking towards a more exciting, albeit distant future, saying, "Even though you've been unfaithful to Me, I am going to woo you back. I will win you back, and together we will honor our betrothal." What God is ultimately saying is that He has a courageous plan to reconcile the marriage—a plan that will unfold in the second episode of the story.

He has a courageous plan to reconcile the marriage.

As episode one continues, the Holy Spirit gives the prophets clearer sneak peeks at this future reconciliation plan. The prophet Isaiah writes: "Though your sins are like scarlet, [though you've cheated like crazy], I will make them as white as snow" (Isa. 1:18, paraphrase). Then later in the book of Isaiah, God gives us even bigger clues:

> *"But he [the Messiah] was pierced for our transgressions, he was crushed for our iniquities; the punishment that brought us peace was upon him, and by his wounds we are healed. We all, like sheep, have gone astray, each of us has turned to his own way [we have gone after false idols]; and the LORD has laid on him [the Messiah, Yeshua] the iniquity of us all" (Isaiah 53:5-6, personal notations in parentheses).*

The New Testament unveils the unconditional nature of God's love for us: "But God demonstrates his own love for us in this: While we were still sinners [cheating on Him], Christ died for us" (Rom. 5:8, personal notations in parentheses). We see that even though God has been cheated on, He loves us so much that He gave up His life to save the marriage.

Isn't that astounding? In our limited, human understanding this seems crazy. God left the comfort of Heaven to atone for our unfaithfulness by coming to Earth so the marriage can be saved. You cannot write a better love story than this. But here's where it really gets good. The story becomes downright thrilling as we look at the parallels between ancient Jewish weddings and God's plan to save His bride from sin.

Ancient Jewish weddings had three significant stages that both the bride and bridegroom had to go through before officially tying the knot. Stage one involved the family of the groom finding a bride and establishing a covenant with her. They established the covenant by signing a ketubah. Stage two was the preparation of the bridal chamber where the consummation of the marriage would take place months later. Stage three was the actual consummation of the marriage and the wedding feast. This weeklong wedding feast was to celebrate the marriage being finalized. This ancient wedding pattern serves as a model for modern, western weddings today. A wedding processional initiates the process; followed by a ceremony, often under a canopy, where the man and the woman are joined together; finally followed by a huge celebration after the ceremony.

Each stage involves several steps to reach completion. Keeping this in mind, it is truly fascinating to see Jesus fulfilling all three parallel stages of a Jewish wedding during the last two episodes of God's great trilogy. I want to highlight a few of these stages to help visualize how the covenant foreshadow is intended to be a beautiful picture of a marriage between God and His people. Highlighting these parallels will no doubt elicit some "a-ha" moments, because you will finally have some context for passages you have surely read many times before.

CHOOSING A BRIDE

The following subtitles for the rest of the chapter are inspired by the book *The Ancient Jewish Wedding* by Jamie Lash.[4]

---

4 Lash, Jamie. (1997). The ancient jewish wedding: And the return of Messiah for his bride. Jewish Jewels.

The first stage of an ancient Jewish wedding was to establish the marriage covenant, and the first step of the marriage covenant involved the family selecting a bride for the groom. Unlike our modern western culture today, arranged marriage was common practice in ancient times and still is in some eastern cultures. The bride would be carefully, intentionally chosen, based on a number of factors. The selection of a bride was sometimes made by the father of the groom, sometimes by the groom himself, and sometimes by both father and son together.

Now consider the parallel, or foreshadow to this custom: the manner in which God has selected each one of us is recorded in Ephesians: "For he chose us in him before the creation of the world to be holy and blameless in his sight" (Eph. 1:4). This verse shows God chose us in Messiah. When did He choose us? Before the creation of the world. Which means God chose His spotless Bride even before He pushed the play button in Genesis 1:1. That means God was thinking about you before He even began writing this story.

THE BRIDE'S PRICE IS ESTABLISHED

The next step in the covenant stage involved paying the bride's family the bride price. In Hebrew, this is called, *mohar*. In the west it is known as a dowry. The bride price was usually paid to the bride's family through the means of something of value such as silver or gold or with the gift of livestock, such as sheep, goats, or chickens. A deal would be negotiated, sometimes including money and livestock—perhaps one hundred shekels, five goats, and twenty chickens. If the deal was acceptable to both parties, they would sign the agreement.

Here's where it gets interesting...

Did you know, Jesus, our Messiah, paid the mohar for us? He paid our bride price, and the New Testament informs us Jesus didn't pay the mohar with silver or gold. He paid it with His own precious blood.

"For you know that it was not with perishable things such as silver or gold that you were redeemed from the empty way of life handed down to you from your forefathers, but with the precious blood of Christ, a lamb without blemish or defect" (1 Peter 1:18-19).

Paul reiterates this in his letter to the Corinthians, which states, "...you were bought at a price..." (1 Cor. 6:20). Yet again, in 1 Corinthians 7:23 we see the apostle reiterate this sentiment, "You were bought at a price; do not become slaves of men."

A LEGAL DOCUMENT IS WRITTEN

Did you know prenuptials were not only commonplace, but expected in ancient Israel's weddings? This marital agreement is not the same thing we see in today's corrupt society. Because of the vulnerability of women in ancient society, this legal document, known as a ketubah, protected the bride's interests more than the groom's.

The agreement included the bride price, of course, but also the bride's rights and the groom's vows to provide for all the bride's needs. The bride and groom were both expected to be faithful and to honor one another in the marriage. This document was a covenant agreement. That should be an "a-ha" moment for you. God's Word is His covenant with His Bride. Like like the ancient Jewish wedding tradition, God's covenant protects us and gives us more security, joy, and love than we could ever imagine. Of course, humankind can, and often does, reject this priceless gift.

THE BRIDE MUST GIVE HER CONSENT

When a bride was chosen, a deal had to be reached between the two families. This stood in contrast to the happenstance meeting of a man and a woman. Now, just to be sure you're understanding this picture clearly, Jesus plainly said to us, "You did not choose me, but

I chose you..." (John 15:16). Scripture unveils it is God who chooses us, just like the bride was chosen in the ancient Jewish wedding tradition.

Even though a deal had been made between two families, it is important to recognize *the bride still had to agree to the marriage.* She had to give her consent for the wedding to move forward, just as Rebekah did with Jacob—as we see in Genesis 24:58: "So they called Rebekah and asked her, 'Will you go with this man?' 'I will go,' she said." Note that when a Jewish woman gave her consent, the couple were considered betrothed, which was as good as being married, although their marriage had not yet been consummated.

There is a parallel here, as this is also true of us as we relate to our Lord. Even though God chooses us we must still give our consent to His proposal. We must say, "I do" in response to God choosing us, which is why scripture tells us, "That if you confess with your mouth, 'Jesus is Lord,' and believe in your heart that God raised him from the dead, you will be saved" (Rom. 10:9). Even though God chooses us, we must still confess Jesus' Lordship with our own mouth, and we must believe in our own heart He is Lord, so we can be saved through our spirit's union with His. We have to accept the covenant. These are two vital steps which we must adhere to have a life-saving relationship with our Bridegroom.

It is important to understand that God never forces Himself on anyone. God chooses us, but we still have a choice to make. We have to choose God too, by saying, "I do." If you have not yet done so, I want you to know, God is pursuing you. Today is a great day to sign a ketubah contract with God.

THE FIRST CUP OF THE COVENANT AND BRIDAL GIFTS

The next step in the first stage of the marriage covenant was a ceremony called, "The First Cup of the Covenant." After the financial negotiation of the marriage had been concluded and the bride had given her consent to the deal, the ketubah was signed. At this point, the bridegroom gave the bride gifts and held up a glass of wine and proclaimed the following blessing: "*Baruch Atah Adonai eluhanu melach Ha-olam boray pree haga-phen*"—translated as: "Blessed are you, O Lord our God, King of the universe who brings forth fruit from the vine."

Next, after having spoken the blessing of the First Cup of the Covenant, the bridegroom would take a sip from the cup and then offer it to his bride. This act was symbolic of the life they would share and the groom would add a closing statement to this effect: "Soon, I will be yours and you will be mine, forever." Following this statement, the bridegroom would depart to prepare the marital residence, and the couple would not see each other for a period of time, sometimes even lasting a whole year.

I am going to give a little spoiler here, but if you have read the account of the last Passover supper for Jesus and His disciples in the gospels, you have probably had another "a-ha" moment. When the couple meets again for the wedding, they will drink a second cup of wine together before the weeklong wedding feast that closes the final ceremony. Remember we are considering how God uses parallels to the ancient Jewish wedding ritual in His betrothal process to us. On the night Jesus was betrayed, He held up the glass of wine during the Passover seder (the Passover feast ritual), and this is what He said to His disciples:

> "*Then he (Yeshua) took the cup, gave thanks and of-fered it to them, saying, 'Drink from it, all of you. This is my blood of the covenant, which is poured out for many for the forgiveness of sins. I tell you, I will not drink of this fruit of the vine from now on until that day when I drink it anew with you in my Father's kingdom'*" (Matthew 26:27-29).

Do you see that perfect parallel? In verse twenty-nine, Jesus has in mind the wedding feast of the Lamb when we will celebrate with our Bridegroom and share the second cup of our covenant.

Can you discern how this language incorporates the reconciliation of the marriage covenant? Within the original covenant, we were unfaithful to God. Jesus remedied this by shedding His blood to atone for our unfaithfulness. This is what He references here, saying, "This is my blood of the covenant..." We ruthlessly trampled on the first one, so this is the new covenant Jesus has established with us. He will not take another sip of wine until the royal wedding feast takes place in the final scene of the last episode. How beautifully orchestrated God's plan is for our redemption.

THE MIKVEH: A RITUAL OF CLEANSING THROUGH WATER IMMERSION

According to the ancient Jewish wedding custom, when the bridegroom had returned to his father's house, the bride would undergo a ritual cleansing—she would take a sanctifying bath in what is called a *Mikveh*. The Mikveh was a bath used for these specific cleansing rituals. The ritual bath in a Mikveh symbolized the bride's new membership into her husband's household. This cleansing ritual indicates the bride's separation from her former way of life, and adoption of her new way of life with her husband.

Now for the covenant foreshadows. I hope you are you ready for another "aha" moment. Remember when Jesus told Nicodemus, a member of the Sanhedrin, "...no one can see the kingdom of God unless he is born again?" (John 3:3). Every person who wishes to enter into the kingdom of God must be born anew. Nicodemus was confused by this, so Jesus explained to him,

"Flesh gives birth to flesh, but the Spirit gives birth to spirit" (John 3:6). What Jesus was directly referencing was a spiritual Mikveh. This is why believers are to be immersed in the name of Jesus. The Mikveh cleanses them from their past and gives them access to their Bridegroom's household or in our parallel, the kingdom of God. When we are baptized, we are saying "I do" to God. Scripture informs us it is the Holy Spirit who immerses us into God through a spiritual baptism (Luke 3:16; Acts 1:5; Acts 11:15-16). It is this spiritual baptism we see foreshadowed in the Mikveh cleansing ritual.

THE BRIDEGROOM DEPARTS TO PREPARE THE CHUPPAH

The next step in the marriage covenant stage is the bridegroom's departure. When all the arrangements have been agreed upon and formalized, the bridegroom will leave his bride-to-be. During this time of separation, one of the groom's primary responsibilities is to prepare the bridal chamber, or chuppah. It is in the bridal chamber that the marriage will be consummated. In ancient times, many young Jewish men continued to live in their parent's home even after they were married, which meant the bridal chamber was often a room in their father's house.

This bridal chamber (chuppah) traditionally functioned not only as a room where the marriage would be consummated, but also as a room the husband and wife would occupy as a living space during their marriage. The Hebrew word, chuppah, is found three times in the Bible. It is a unique word that is used to describe a canopy under which Jewish wedding ceremonies are performed today. This type of covering, just like the bridegroom's prepared chamber for his bride, conveys a sense of privacy, intimacy, and protection. Under the chuppah, the betrothed couple finds safe refuge from the harsh realities of the outside world.

In the book of Joel, we discover one of three texts where the term chuppah is used: "Let the bridegroom leave his room and the bride her chamber" (Joel 2:16). The word, "chamber" reflects the Hebrew word, chuppah. This chamber was a place of privacy and refuge for the bride.

We are safe under the shelter of the Lord Almighty, and we are at liberty to bask in His glory.

My favorite use of the word chuppah, however, comes from a passage in Isaiah. In this passage, God says He will create a special chuppah for the Israelites on Mount Zion—where the Temple Mount is located in Jerusalem and serves as ground zero or the starting point or base for God's covenant activity. This is the place God chose as a refuge for the Israelites from the harsh elements of life. Mount Zion was chosen several thousand years ago and the profound beauty of this special protective canopy is that God is the actual Chuppah. This particular Chuppah consists of God's Shekinah glory. Scripture presents a striking picture of God's Shekinah glory:

> *"Then the LORD will create over all of Mount Zion and over those who assemble there a cloud of smoke by day and a glow of flaming fire by night; over all the glory will be a canopy [chuppah]. It will be a shelter and shade from the heat of the day, and a refuge and hiding place from the storm and rain" (Isa. 4:5-6).*

What a powerful picture of how our Bridegroom cares for us. God is our shelter and our refuge from the storms of life; He is our Chuppah. The chuppah is a stunning picture of God's love for us. It illustrates His longing for intimacy with us and conveys how He has taken the lead in providing us with His protection. We are safe under the shelter of the Lord Almighty, and we are at liberty to bask in His glory.

During that last Passover supper, shortly before Jesus was crucified, He and His disciples shared a meal and Jesus had washed their feet. In this intimate setting, Jesus said:

> *"In my Father's house are many rooms; if it were not so, I would have told you. I am going there to prepare a place for you. And if I go and prepare a place for you, I will come back and take you to be with me that you also may be where I am" (John 14:2-3).*

Look at the first sentence: Jesus refers to many "rooms" in His Father's house. In the New Testament, the Greek word for "rooms" is used, but Jesus most likely used the Hebrew word, chuppah. He was Jewish, and given the intimate setting where this passage occurs, with His Jewish disciples, He almost certainly spoke Hebrew or Aramaic.

Although Jesus was speaking to His disciples, the Bible is God's Word and was written for every person who says, "I do" to God's call. So, Jesus explains He is going to prepare a chuppah, and goes on to say, "...if it were not so, I would have told you. I am going there to prepare a place for you. And if I go and prepare a place for you, I will come back and take you to be with me that you also may be where I am."

In light of the ancient Jewish wedding tradition, when we understand the subtle nuances of what Jesus actually means, His words can be interpreted as romantically-charged language. We can easily recognize Jesus has the bridal chamber in view of where our marriage will one day be finalized in New Jerusalem. Until this date set in the future, our Groom is preparing the bridal chamber for us.

It will be a loving, safe, intimate place where we will be protected from the harsh elements of the outside world. There will be no more pain, tears, suffering, or death.

Hopefully, you now understand why followers of Jesus are often referred to as the Bride of Christ[5] or the Bride of Messiah. And while I know the nature of the Bridegroom and Bride's consummation is spiritual, I imagine Jesus will spare nothing to make it an eternal night to remember. Until then, as the Bride, we are waiting for our beloved Groom to appear. The Hebrew phrase, *Bo Adonia Yeshua* means "Come, Lord Jesus," written in Greek as *Maranatha*. This is our eternal hope.

THE BRIDE IS SET APART IN WAITING

In the ancient Jewish tradition, the bride had no idea when the groom would return. She certainly could not wear her wedding dress every day for an entire year. This is why Jesus told the parable of the ten virgins (Matt. 25:1-13). The Bride asks ten of her virgin friends to go out and watch for the Bridegroom. The idea was for them to wait until they heard Him coming with His entourage, and then to go out and meet Him so the Bride could quickly dress and prepare herself before the Bridegroom's arrival.

> God is our shelter and our refuge from the storms of life; He is our Chuppah.

What is very interesting here is the timing of the bridegroom's return for his bride, as the timing was most often left up to his father. This had the effect of keep-

5 Fruchtebaum, Arnold. (2013 revised). *The Footsteps of the Messiah*, p.cm. Originally published: San Antonio, TX: Ariel Press c 1982.

ing the son in an enthusiastic suspense as well as he did not know when the big day would arrive. The parallel here is very clear. When speaking about the time of His return, Jesus said: "No one knows about that day or hour, not even the angels in heaven, nor the Son, but only the Father" (Matt. 24:36). These words spoken by Jesus, coupled with the parable of the ten virgins, presents us with the concept we are to remain faithful, holy, and pure while doing the work of the Kingdom of God as we wait for Messiah's return. But what will happen when He returns? In 2 Peter 3:10,14, we explore a powerful reminder of what is to come:

> *"But the day of the Lord will come like a thief. The heavens will disappear with a roar; the elements will be destroyed by fire, and the earth and everything in it will be laid bare.... So then, dear friends, since you are looking forward to this, make every effort to be found spotless, blameless and at peace with him."*

Jesus is, without a doubt, coming back for us. When He does it will be in extraordinary power. This is when our indomitable King will truly display His royalty, and omnipotence.

"But," you may ask, "what is He doing in the meantime?" This astonishing foreshadow allows us to focus on a magnificent hope in God while we work and we wait. Our mighty Bridegroom has promised to return for us after He works with our Father to prepare our eternal home.

But what has to happen before moving into a family home? A majestic, no-expenses-spared, over-the-top royal wedding, of course. As you might have guessed, this all takes place in the third episode of the Covenant. And I say it is a magnificent hope because it is more than you could imagine in your wildest dreams. Let us see what this royal wedding entails.

CHAPTER 6

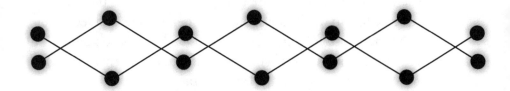

Covenant, Episode No. 3: The Wedding

"And so we will be with the Lord forever."
—1 Thessalonians 4:17

The last two chapters have prepared us for the third and most exciting episode of The Covenant which is the royal wedding. We know Mashiach returns in episode three and brings us right to the wedding ceremony in New Jerusalem. God has reconciled the marriage, Jesus has ascended into Heaven, the bridal chamber has been prepared, and He will be coming back to claim His Bride with a blast of the shofar and a triumphant shout. We have covered several of the stages that occur before the wedding ceremony, but let's quickly recap the last couple of foreshadows that transition to episode three, the royal wedding.

THE PREPARATION OF THE CHUPPAH

Because the day and the hour were unknown, the bridegroom had to wait for his father to declare that it was time to get the bride just as the bride had to wait unknowingly for her groom's sudden arrival. This element of the unknown greatly added to the excitement and also kept the bride from becoming distracted or perhaps even unfaithful. We see this parallel in Mark's gospel:

> *"No one knows about that day or hour, not even the angels in heaven, nor the Son, but only the Father. Be on guard! Be alert! You do not know when that time will come. It's like a man going away: He leaves his house and puts his servants in charge, each with his assigned task, and tells the one at the door to keep watch. Therefore keep watch because you do not know when the owner of the house will come back—whether in the evening, or at midnight, or when the rooster crows, or at dawn. If he comes suddenly, do not let him find you sleeping. What I say to you, I say to everyone: 'Watch!'"* (Mark 13:32-37).

As the bridegroom worked hard on preparing his bride's chuppah, the bride eagerly awaited his return, knowing her betrothed could arrive at any time, even at midnight. Therefore, she had to be ready at all times while carrying out her specific role in the Master's household. Jesus also referred to this in the parable of the ten virgins, recorded in Matthew 25:1-13. In both these examples, Jesus emphasizes that we are not simply waiting for His return. He intends for us to be taking care of God's household and winning more people into His kingdom.

THE BRIDEGROOM RETURNS WITH A SHOFAR AND A SHOUT

As we saw in chapter five, when the bridegroom had departed, the bride was consecrated (set apart or sanctified) for the period of time during which the bridegroom was away building the marital home. If the bridegroom was planning to remain in his father's house with his new bride, he would be away from her preparing the bridal chamber. We see a parallel to this custom depicted in Revelation: "I saw the Holy City, the new Jerusalem, coming down out of heaven from God, prepared as a bride beautifully dressed for her husband" (Rev. 21:2).

Of course, the implication in this final scene in God's story is that believers are identified with New Jerusalem. Jerusalem was, is, and will always be God's prize. She is the center of the universe and the only place where several times in scripture, God says He has placed His name forever.

> *"...In this temple and in Jerusalem, which I have chosen out of all the tribes of Israel, I will put my Name forever" (2 Kings 21:7).*

Jerusalem has been through a lot of tribulation in her history because of her rebelliousness. She has been trampled on by nation after nation. However, God has a plan to redeem Jerusalem from the consequences of her rebelliousness forever, just as He has a plan to redeem us from ours forever. Revelation 21:2 presents a beautiful picture of the Holy City as the redeemed, unstained, purified Bride of Messiah Jesus, covered by His blood, coming down from Heaven, prepared as a bride. And as we will soon see, this is also a picture of the ultimate wedding processional that will lead to the consummation of the marriage.

Before the bridegroom could go and call for his bride, the bridegroom's father had to be satisfied his son had made every preparation. Only when the groom's father was satisfied would he officially give his son permission to go and call for his bride. For this reason, Jesus said, "No one knows about that day or hour, not even the angels in heaven, nor the Son, but only the

Father" (Matt. 24:36).

As was the ancient custom, the bridegroom would return around midnight and upon his arrival he would be announced with a shout. This is relayed in the parable of the ten virgins as follows: "At midnight the cry rang out: 'Here's the bridegroom! Come out to meet him!'" (Matt. 25:6). When his arrival had been boldly announced, a ram's horn (shofar) would be blown. We find a parallel for this ancient custom in scripture:

> *"For the Lord himself will come down from heaven, with a loud command, with the voice of the archangel and with the trumpet call of God, and the dead in Christ (Messiah) will rise first. After that, we who are still alive and are left will be caught up together with them in the clouds to meet the Lord in the air. And so we will be with the Lord forever" (1 Thess. 4:16-17).*

Can you see the foreshadows here? This passage of scripture gives us a precise understanding of how our royal Bridegroom will arrive with a loud shout and a trumpet call initiated by God, our Father. In Jewish antiquity, when the father of the bridegroom gave his son the order to go and collect his bride, the son would gather together all his friends and family from the town he lived in and they would form a huge processional. It would turn into a festive party with singing and shouting and the blowing of shofars all along the way until they reached the bride's home.

THE CONSUMMATION OF THE MARRIAGE

When the bridegroom reached the bride's house, it was time for the marriage to be consummated in the chuppah. The blood-stained linen from this night was preserved to show proof of the bride's virginity. This custom is referenced in Deuteronomy

22:13-21. Typically, the friend of the bridegroom (the best man) would wait outside the room to receive word from the groom proclaiming the marriage had been consummated. Here is another fascinating foreshadow: John the baptizer was most likely referencing this tradition in John's gospel, saying:

> *"You yourselves can testify that I said, 'I am not the Christ (Messiah) but am sent ahead of him.' The bride belongs to the bridegroom. The friend who attends the bridegroom waits and listens for him, and is full of joy when he hears the bridegroom's voice. That joy is mine, and it is now complete" (John 3:28-29).*

Isn't that amazing? John was announcing that the second episode of God's trilogy had begun with the ministry of Jesus as he recognized the voice of the Messiah. His joy was full because he saw God's master plan was unfolding as He willed it to. Imagine John's excitement when he saw a vision of the great wedding and consummation that will take place in the third and final episode of God's story. He probably experienced a vision of that final wedding celebration and my guess is that it was quite the party.

Just like our ancient wedding covenant foreshadow, after having received the signal from the friend of the Bridegroom regarding consummation of the marriage, great rejoicing will break out as the New Jerusalem wedding celebration becomes a grand party.

THE SECOND CUP OF THE COVENANT AND THE MARRIAGE SUPPER

After the announcement that the marriage had been consummated, the couple would leave their wedding chamber to join the party. Since they had consummated the marriage, the happy couple would then drink their second cup of the covenant to-gether. If you remember, this is the foreshadow Jesus was referencing when He said He would not drink of the fruit of the vine again until we were with Him in His Father's kingdom. The next and final step in the wedding celebration is the majestic and bountiful wedding feast. It is a weeklong celebration with plenty of food, dancing, and wine. Remember the first miracle in John's gospel, when Jesus attended the wedding in Cana, and the hosts ran out of wine towards the end of the week? Prompted by His mother, Mary, Jesus turned four barrels of water into fine wine, and this was at the end of the wedding feast. Jews sure do know how to celebrate.

As we know, the great marriage feast in New Jerusalem will not be a weeklong party, it will be an eternal party that never ends and never runs out of wine. We will finally ride off into the sunset to live happily ever after with our great Hero and Lover. Take a look at the final wedding feast mentioned in Revelation:

> *"Then I heard what sounded like a great multitude, like the roar of rushing waters and like loud peals of thunder, shouting: 'Hallelujah! For our Lord God Almighty reigns. Let us rejoice and be glad and give him glory! For the wedding of the Lamb has come, and his bride has made herself ready. Fine linen, bright and clean, was given her to wear.' [Fine linen stands for the righteous acts of the saints.] Then the angel said to me, 'Write: 'Blessed are those who are invited to the wedding supper of the Lamb!' ' And he added, 'These are the true words of God'" (Rev. 19:6-9).*

Isn't this another inspiring parallel to the final step in wedding celebrations practiced throughout Jewish antiquity? God's court-ship of His people will culminate in a grand, New Jerusalem wedding. Here we see God's Covenant love story with His people in its entire glory and splendor as foreshadowed by His covenant with Israel. This is the covenant foreshadow, and guess what, it is still only the first one. There are six more and they all unfold the same way, and ultimately point to the spiritual reality we will experience in episode three of God's trilogy.

As we conclude this chapter, I hope God's unconditional love for you is apparent. No matter how far we stray from God, He never strays from us. God never stops pursuing us, never gives up on us, never stops having our best interest in mind, and He never stops waiting for us to return to Him. Like the father in the story of the prodigal son, God anxiously waits and waits no matter how long it takes. And then when we return, He throws a wild party to celebrate. His love is authentic and everlasting. The Covenant Foreshadow is a beautiful picture of God's never-ending commitment to us. He is a promise-keeper and will remain faithful even when we are unfaithful:

> "Here is a trustworthy saying: If we died with him, we will also live with him; if we endure, we will also reign with him. If we disown him, he will also disown us; if we are faithless, he remains faithful, for he cannot disown himself" (2 Tim. 2:11-13).

PART III

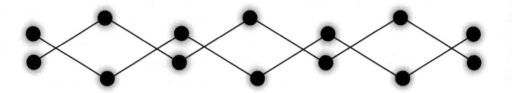

CHAPTER 7

The Nation of Israel, Episode No. 1: One Nation under God

*"Family is where our story begins
and love never ends"
—Author unknown*

One of the most alluring, yet challenging, features of God's story is dealing with the erratic nature of human relationships. The foreshadow we are about to explore—the nation of Israel—dramatically underscores this reality. In the first chapter of Genesis, we read that God created everything we see in the universe. It took God six days to complete this work then, like all creatives, God stood back to admire His work. He was so pleased he said, "Oh I like this, what we have created is good. It's really good..." (Paraphrase of Gen. 1:31).

Just a few verses later, God observed something was not good. After God created Adam, He said, "... It is not good for the man to be alone..." (Gen. 2:18). This statement stands in contrast to the rest of the goodness of creation. Could it perhaps be a clue to the reason for creation? Why was it not good for Adam to be alone? I believe since God created us to be in a relationship, we are essentially incomplete on our own. To help Adam understand his need for relationship, God did not create Eve right away, although He had already decided to "...make a helper suitable for him" (Gen. 2:18).

Instead of creating Eve immediately, God first arranged for all the animals to come to Adam to be named. Note that this was a real job with real authority. Whatever name Adam chose became the official name for that animal, whether it was a hippopotamus, an orangutan, or an armadillo. At some point in the naming process, Adam most likely realized there were males and females of each species but there existed no female counterpart for him. No partner with whom Adam could share life's most intimate and precious moments. No equal to explore the world with. There was no one with whom to build hopes and dreams, or to build a family legacy.

Scripture then tells us that God created Eve from Adam's rib (See Genesis 2:22). Notice the manner in which God created Eve underscores the intimate connection she and Adam shared. It also emphasizes the interdependent bond they would develop, having become *basar echad*, which is Hebrew for "one flesh." When Adam woke up he was surprised beyond belief. The first words he blurted were: "This is now bone of my bones, and flesh of my flesh..." (Gen. 2:23). At which point he gives his new counterpart the generic classification *Isha*, which is Hebrew for "woman" because she came from *Ish*, which is Hebrew for "man." This was no doubt an exhilarating moment for Adam as he began to imagine their future together. Nonetheless, it is also easy to imagine God, standing off to one side, thinking, *Buddy, you have no idea what you two are in for.*

Sadly, it was not long before the honeymoon was over. The wheels came off for the newlyweds when they ate the forbidden fruit in the garden. The consequence of disobeying God was their eviction from the garden. This brought an abrupt end to their comfortable life and the security of paradise. Adam and Eve were suddenly on the wrong side of the knowledge of good and evil. Not only did they have to toil for their food, but they also toiled in their relationships. And as a result of Adam and Eve's sin, humankind has been toiling for its food and relationships ever since.

Shortly after their expulsion from paradise, Adam and Eve had two little boys. They became young men, but they could not escape the curse of damaged relationships. The unimaginable happened when the older brother murdered the younger. From this terrible moment onward, human relationships degenerated into messy, tangled, and hopelessly sinful affairs until God finally said, "Enough." By orchestrating a catastrophic flood, God wiped the almost entirely corrupt human race from the face of the Earth. Only one righteous man and his family were spared. His name was Noah. From the seed of Noah, humanity received a fresh, new start. Four hundred years after Noah, a man named Abram was born. He was chosen by God to be the father of a special new family that ultimately became known as the nation of Israel.

After many twists and turns, this special family was given a home called "The Promised Land," set in a very specific region of the world, which will be explored in the next chapter. They were also given a very specific set of family rules, called the Torah. These rules would become the gold standard for how to love God, how to love oneself, how to love each other, and how to love the rest of the world in radical ways. Having a family home enabled them to practice the family rules they needed to keep them safe. And like all the other foreshadows in this series, this gold standard for relationship progresses in all three episodes of God's story. It begins as one nation under God in the first episode of God's story, expands to one new man under God in the second episode, and finally, into one multitude under God in the third episode, the final chapter of God's story.

To begin with episode one, the nation of Israel lived according to the rules of a theocracy when it was first given possession of The Promised Land. This was to be theocracy in which God would be their invisible King, they would be His very visible subjects, and the Torah would be their constitution. In Exodus, God says to the nation of Israel:

> *"Now if you obey me fully and keep my covenant, then out of all nations you will be my treasured possession. Although the whole earth is mine, you will be for me a kingdom of priests and a holy nation...." (Exod. 19:5–6)*

The word "holy" as seen here means to be "set apart." Under this theocracy, the people of Israel would live their daily lives in a manner that was different from the other nations of the Earth. When they entered into this covenant with God, the Israelites dressed in a manner different from other nations. Also, the food they ate was different. The principles governing their work was different. The nation of Israel would raise their children in a manner that differed from the nations surrounding them, and most importantly, the way they worshiped one God would be different. The way in which they expressed their love had to be different from how the rest of the entire world expressed its love.

From this point in the story to the beginning of the second episode, God separated the world population into only two people groups. He described these groups using two terms: the *Yehudim* (the Hebrew term for Jews) and the *Goyim* (the Hebrew term for Gentiles, or the nations). This distinction made Israel witnesses to the rest of the nations, as Israel lived out a totally new and radical form of love. It was a love that would develop from them keeping all 613 of the commandments, or family rules, found in the Torah.

Matthew's gospel records how Jesus was once ap-proached by a Torah teacher, and asked:

"'Teacher, which is the greatest commandment in the Law?' Jesus replied: 'Love the Lord your God with all your heart and with all your soul and with all your mind. This is the first and greatest commandment. And the second is like it: Love your neighbor as your-self" (Matt. 22:36-39).

Jesus followed this and said something truly remarkable: "All the Law and the Prophets hang on these two commandments [in Hebrew pronounced *mitzvot*]" (Matt. 22:40).

Jesus is saying the entire Bible can be condensed into two radi-cal forms of love: first, radical ways to love God, and second, rad-ical ways to love others. Israel's tangible demonstration of their love for God and others was therefore solely built upon their faithful observance of the Torah.

Through this radical, yet loving theocratic relationship, Israel would become a witness to the Gentile nations. The world would witness something it had never seen before—an entire nation of people loving God and loving others in radical ways. It was new to the whole world. It was radical in the sense that it affected the fundamental nature of how love was perceived. Through Israel, God changed the way love had been perceived prior to that point in human history. The Jewish people were instructed to set them-selves apart from the rest of the world by observing special days and seasons, by taking care of those who are poor and powerless, by conducting business in ethical ways, and by altering their diet and appearance as symbols of belonging to God and willfully sub-mitting to His authority.

It was a win-win system for the Yehudim (the Jewish people) and the Goyim (the nations.) Jewish people were to shine like a bright light for other nations to follow. Unfortunately, though, because we are all imperfect humans, the Jewish people failed in their ability to keep God's high moral and ethical standards. Abraham's family's storyline ends up reading more like a stranger-than-fiction soap opera than it does a model family for the world.

The storyline would include heart-wrenching drama such as rape, incest, adultery, sexual addiction, deceit, theft, insurrection, and again, even murder. As if these deviations were not bad enough, Israel often neglected to take care of the people closest to God's heart—the poor, the powerless, and the marginalized. As scripture often illustrates, selfishness ruled and people did what was right in their own eyes. As the family story progressed, Isaiah gave us a great insight into how God felt about Israel's failings. In the passage below, notice how God continues with the theme of a jilted lover. Consider the previous examples of this theme as God uses the poetic metaphor of a vineyard to describe His troubled relationship with Israel:

> *"I will sing for the one I love a song about his vineyard: My loved one had a vineyard on a fertile hillside. He dug it up and cleared it of stones and planted it with the choicest vines. He built a watchtower in it and cut out a winepress as well. Then he looked for a crop of good grapes, but it yielded only bad fruit. 'Now you dwellers in Jerusalem and men of Judah, judge between me and my vineyard. What more could have been done for my vineyard than I have done for it? When I looked for good grapes, why did it yield only bad? Now I will tell you what I am going to do to my vineyard: I will take away its hedge, and it will be destroyed; I will break down its wall, and it will be trampled. I will make it a wasteland, neither pruned nor cultivated, and briers and thorns will grow there. I will command the clouds not to rain on it.' The vineyard of the LORD Almighty*

is the house of Israel, and the men of Judah are the garden of his delight. And he looked for justice, but saw bloodshed; for righteousness, but heard cries of distress" (Isa. 5:1-7).

According to this passage, God did all He could to create a fertile environment for a healthy, choice crop of grapes. Israel, however, failed to maintain their side of the relationship, managing only to produce a crop of bad grapes.

Not one vine was seen to yield the fruit of justice. Instead, there was only bloodshed. Not one vine was seen to yield the root of righteousness. Instead, there was only cries of distress. It is another sad turning point in the story as God's Bride (Israel) fails again to love Him properly. Further, Israel failed dismally at loving members of their own nation and the other nations of the world. Israel failed to love in the radical ways God designed for their love to be expressed. As a disciplinary consequence of their continuous, monumental failure, God exiled the family of Israel from their promised home to a brutal, pagan land called Babylon. God was faithful to return Israel to their land seventy years later, yet the lesson still was not learned. A second exile—or scattering—would be necessary later on in the story, when Israel persisted in her disobedience to God.

From what we learned in The Covenant foreshadow, we know

God was faithful to return Israel to their land seventy years later, yet the lesson still was not learned...

God vowed to faithfully keep the promises He made to Israel, even when she was unfaithful to Him. The good news is, He will bring her back to The Promised Land towards the end of the story. This is the part we are currently witnessing in our own lifetime.

We see in Isaiah just one of many passages referencing God's promise to gather the Jewish people back into The Promised Land, after they had been scattered to the four corners of the Earth during the second exile:

> *"In that day [the day we are living in right now] the Lord will reach out his hand a second time [the first time was the Babylonian exile 607 BC, and the second was the Roman exile AD 70] to reclaim the remnant that is left of his people from Assyria, from Lower Egypt, from Upper Egypt, from Cush, from Elam, from Babylonia, from Hamath and from the islands of the sea. He will raise a banner for the nations and gather the exiles of Israel; he will assemble the scattered people of Judah from the four quarters of the earth" (Isa. 11:11-12).*

It is an astonishing prophecy because after being exiled from their family home for almost 2,000 years, God has returned His beloved Israel to their home. Israel officially became a sovereign state again on May 14, 1948. Jews from all around the world have continued to return in large numbers to their homeland each year ever since.

Next, let's take look at how God's wonderful and mysterious plan is unveiled in episode two, as the Gentile nations are included in His plan for Israel.

CHAPTER 8

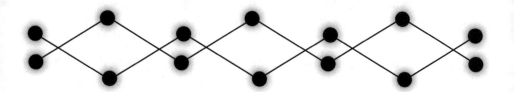

The Nation of Israel, Episode No. 2: One New Man under God

D espite what we may believe, God has always had a plan to help Israel produce good grapes. His plan was to promote Israel from one nation under God in the first episode, to one new man under God in the second. In a unexpected twist for Israel at that time, God did this by placing Jews and Gentiles (Yehudim and Goyim) on an equal spiritual level. In the passage below we are introduced to the advent of spiritual equality through faith in the Messiah. However, first we are reminded about the former exclusion of the Gentiles:

"Therefore, remember that formerly you who are Gentiles [Goyim] by birth and called 'uncircumcised' by those who call themselves 'the circumcision' (that done in the body by the hands of men)— remember that at

that time you were separate from Christ [Messiah], excluded from citizenship in Israel and foreigners to the covenants of the promise, without hope and without God in the world" (Eph. 2:11-12).

One of the major problems in the first episode was that Israel's Torah observance often created an us-against-them kind of mentality. This was often due to how some Jewish people kept the Torah. As seen in the passage above, Paul explains how circumcision was being used to that end. Those who were circumcised (the Jews) were members of the club, and those who had not been circumcised (the Gentiles) were refused membership, unless they became circumcised and began keeping all the commandments (mitzvot) in the Torah.

Instead of enriching the world with a radically new form of love that would draw the other nations to God, the nation of Israel often segregated the world with a radical form of religious conformity. Rather than loving their neighbors as themselves, ancient Israel isolated themselves from their neighbors in perceived superiority.

God, through the teaching of the Torah, was very clear about how the Israelites were to love the foreigners in their midst:

"The alien living with you must be treated as one of your native-born. Love him as yourself, for you were aliens in Egypt. I am the LORD your God" (Lev. 19:34).

When Jesus told the parable of the good Samaritan, He specifically targeted this kind of exclusionary posture. An expert in the law stood up on one occasion to test Jesus asking Him what he should do to inherit eternal life. Recognizing the man's hidden motive, Jesus asked him what is written in the Torah. The expert answered, "...'Love the Lord your God with all your heart and with all your soul and with all your strength and with all your mind'; and, 'Love your neighbor as yourself'" (Luke 10:27). Jesus told him he had answered correctly adding, "Do this and you will live" (Luke 10:28).

Scripture tells us the man wanted to justify himself so he asked Jesus, "And who is my neighbor?" (Luke 10:29). In spite of the man's innocent question, Jesus clearly understood the man's true intention, which was actually to ask, "Does this really mean that everybody in the world is my neighbor?" Yet, this is precisely what Jesus did mean. And He went on to tell the parable of the good Samaritan, hoping to reverse exclusionary thinking.

We can reach the conclusion that circumcision was just one of many ways a Jewish person, in ancient times, could say to a Gentile, "You are not part of this insider club, therefore you are not my neighbor. Therefore I am not required to love you as myself."

Now, it is important to remember that Christianity was an all-Jewish movement for the first forty years of its history. Jesus' early Jewish followers had absolutely no intention of starting a new religion called Christianity. They were Jews who believed the promised Messiah had arrived and to them it was the fulfillment of Judaic Prophecy. Even the Jews who did not believe Jesus was the Messiah viewed them, not as a new religion, but as one of many Jewish sects that existed back then. These first followers of Messiah, Yeshua, remained faithful Torah-observant Jews, just as they had been before. Unfortunately, this initially included keeping themselves separate from the Gentiles. We will go more into detail about their Torah observance during the chapter on the Torah foreshadow.

He made it clear to the followers of Yeshua that they were no longer to practice a culture of exclusion.

When God promoted Israel from one nation under God to one new man under God in the second episode of His story, however, He made it clear to the followers of Yeshua that they were no longer to practice a culture of exclusion. We see this development taking place in the Book of Acts. The apostle, Peter, a Jewish disciple, was staying at the home of a Jewish tanner in the city of Joppa (pronounced Yafo in Hebrew). He was praying up on the roof, feeling hungry, and waiting for a delicious kosher lunch to be served, when he fell into a deep, spiritual trance. While in this state, he had a vision of a large sheet being lowered to Earth from Heaven, and on this sheet he saw all kinds of "unclean" animals. The birds, animals, and reptiles he saw were considered forbidden for a Jew to eat—animals God had specified as unclean. Then a voice spoke to Peter saying to him, "Get up, Peter. Kill and eat" (Acts 10:13).

Peter's immediate response was, "Surely not, Lord... I have never eaten anything impure or unclean" (Acts 10:14). Peter told God he had strictly followed the Torah since birth and in that regard implied he was not about to deviate from this strict observance. But then God said, "Do not call anything impure that God has made clean" (Acts 10:15).

The sheet was lowered down to Earth three times in total, leaving Peter feeling puzzled. He was contemplating the meaning of his vision when the Spirit of the Lord told him to accompany the men who were looking for him. At that very moment some men arrived asking for Peter. The men explained they were sent by a holy angel to bring Peter back to the home of a Gentile named Cornelius. At this point, I imagine Peter began to grasp the scope of his vision.

The next day, Peter accompanied these men to the city of Caesarea, about a day's walk, directly north of Yafo. He entered the home of Cornelius, who had invited many other Gentile relatives and friends to join him. This was almost certainly the first time Peter had ever been in the home of a Gentile. At some point after receiving the Torah, the ancient rabbis—not God—taught that Gentiles were unclean and by entering a Gentile home a Jew would be defiled. It is most likely due to this teaching that Peter made the following statement once he had entered the home of Cornelius: "...'You are well aware that it is against our law for a Jew to associate with a Gentile or visit him [again, this was only against rabbinic law]. But God has shown me that I should not call any man impure or unclean'" (Acts 10:28).

As Peter recounted the events of the previous day, the Holy Spirit fell on the Gentiles in the room and they began to speak in other tongues, just like the Jewish believers experienced in the upper room on the day of Pentecost (the feast of Shavuot). The overwhelming message received by Jewish Peter, and every Gentile in the room, is God's glorious truth that the Goyim, the nations, are not excluded from the great gift of salvation by faith and the Holy Spirit.

This was certainly a game-changing moment. Having gained a better understanding of how this elitist club mentality had developed and how it influenced the decision about who was in and who was out, we can now have a look at the rest of Paul's teaching in Ephesians on the subject of exclusion as opposed to inclusion:

> *"Remember that at that time you were separate from Christ (Messiah), excluded from citizenship in Israel and foreigners to the covenants of the promise, without hope and without God in the world. But now in Christ Jesus (Messiah Yeshua) you who once were far away have been brought near through the blood of Christ (Messiah), For he himself is our peace, who has made the two one and has destroyed the barrier, the dividing wall of hostility, by abolishing in his flesh the law with its commandments and regulations. His purpose was to create in himself one new man out of the two, thus making peace, and in this one body to reconcile both*

*of them to God through the cross, by which he put to
death their hostility" (Eph. 2:12-16).*

The concept Paul refers to as "one new man" is a great posture
to adopt. It is an attitude or frame of mind that embraces conflu-
ence—the merging of two separate streams as they become one
stream. Just like in a marriage, where two unique individuals are
joined together to become *basar echad* or one flesh, and are still
able to maintain their unique identities, through faith in Yeshua,
Jews and Gentiles can join together to become one new man while
still maintaining their unique identities.

Biblical records assure us that this is the way things originally
worked when this profound movement of faith began two thousand years ago. When Gentiles came to faith in Jesus, there were
some Jewish followers of Jesus who insisted the Gentiles had to be
circumcised and keep the Torah if they wanted to be part of this
righteous club. But the believing Jewish leaders were careful not
to force the Gentiles to follow this protocol. They knew it was important for Jews to keep their Jewish identity intact, just as it was
for the Gentiles to keep their Gentile identity intact.

Becoming the one new man did not mean there was nothing
left to differentiate themselves from each other. They did not suddenly become one homogenous group. What made them one new
man was their faith in the Messiah. This is the means through
which they were justified. It was not by being circumcised or by
keeping the Torah. Faith in the Messiah is what gave the Jews and
Gentiles an equal footing. This truth was succinctly expressed by
Peter at the Jerusalem Council, recorded in Acts: "He made no
distinction between us (Yehudim) and them (Goyim), for he purified their hearts by faith" (Acts 15:9). Before long, a new segrega-
tion began to affect even this radical new commandment of love.

Years later, as Christianity shifted from an all-Jewish leadership
to an all-Gentile leadership, Christianity's center moved from Jerusalem to Rome. When its Jewish roots shifted to an overwhelm-

ingly Romanized faith, these largely political Gentile leaders made the tragic mistake of forcing Jews to give up that which made them uniquely Jewish. Keeping the Torah, observing Shabbat and other celebrations of the Lord's appointed times (the feasts) became increasingly difficult for all Jews, whether they believed in Jesus or not. Many Jews throughout this time in history were imprisoned, banished, and executed for failing to comply. One can only imagine the insult and dilemma this presented to faithful Jews, not to mention that these restrictive edicts promoted much of the Judeo-Christian antagonism we see today. Perhaps the greatest tragedy of this reversed exclusion was the beauty of the one new man was lost for the next 1,700 years as Christianity became an exclusive club for Gentiles. How ironic. Before he could become a member of this club, a Jew would have to stop being Jewish.

Yet when the Gentiles first came to faith in Jesus the question was, "Do we make them Jews?"

After the Jerusalem Council had debated this question, the answer given was, "No. We want them to retain their Gentile identity."

When the Roman-influenced Christian faith had gained enough momentum, the question became, "What do we do with these Jews?"

The answer, unfortunately was, "Force them to stop being Jewish."

Apart from isolating Jews and placing obstacles in their path to finding the Messiah, the Church was also adversely affected by losing the benefit of Jewish understanding. The Church lost connection to its Jewish roots, which caused her to veer off track. The Church also lost its Jewish understanding regarding the Lord's appointed times (also colloquially known as the "Feasts of the Lord"). Losing the knowledge of how Jesus is foreshadowed in the Lord's appointed times has been a great loss for the Church. When you understand how these appointed times unfold over history and what their spiritual significance is throughout the year, it greatly deepens and strengthens your faith. We will cover this in great detail when we get to the Feast foreshadow.

What is even more disheartening, because of this reverse-exclusionist error, is that we see few Jews come to faith in Jesus for the next 1,700 years. Some came willingly, but most converted under intimidation or by the threat of death. All were made to relinquish their unique Jewish identity. The good news is the Church is finally waking up to this tragic error and knowledge of the "one-new-man" paradigm and a re-establishment to its Jewish roots are making a comeback. This happens in accordance with God's perfect timing as believers worldwide prepare to launch into the exhilarating episode three, where God raises the stakes.

CHAPTER 9

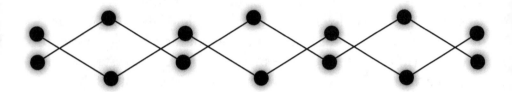

The Nation of Israel, Episode No. 3: One New Multitude under God

W e have established that the nation of Israel moved from one nation under God in episode one to one new man under God in episode two. In the third and final episode, we see a powerful shift from one new man under God to one new *multitude* under God:

> *"After this I looked and there before me was a great multitude that no one could count, from every nation, tribe, people and language, standing before the throne and in front of the Lamb. They were wearing white robes and were holding palm branches in their hands. And they cried out in a loud voice: 'Salvation belongs to our God, who sits on the throne, and to the Lamb'"* (Rev. 7:9–10).

This scene is from the last chapter of the story and it depicts a segment of John's vision into a heavenly future. Notice there is no longer mention of Jew or Gentile, but only a multitude from every nation, tribe, people, and language. This is God's ultimate purpose. God's use of foreshadows throughout the first two episodes is His method of unveiling the mystery of His plan to establish an eternal family. This is where we are headed. The beauty of this vision is the exquisite diversity encompassed within God's eternal family. We won't all look the same and we won't all act in a uniform, cloned manner. We won't have shared the same ethnic tongue on Earth. We will be an eclectic and diverse group of people with diverse functions in the Body of Messiah. I look forward to this day with great anticipation.

Now, regarding Israel beginning as one nation under God, I want to clarify a point: America has never truly been one nation under God. America has never been a theocracy or a system of government in which God is recognized as King and priests typically rule in His name. The commonwealth of Israel operated as a theocracy from the time of Moses until the election of Saul as their king. The American Founding Fathers purposely did not want to create a theocracy. Instead, they created America to be a place of religious freedom. This was their intended purpose no matter what faith an individual practiced. The founders did, of course, lean towards Christianity, but the only theocratic nation under one true God was the nation of Israel.

America has never truly been one nation under God.

Israel began as one nation under God and then transitioned into one new man under God. This new submission is also a theocracy, but it's an *individual* theocracy because each believer willfully submits himself to live under God's authority. It is in this individual theocracy that we finally move to one multitude under God meaning that every nation, tongue, and tribe are together under Him. Again, the theme of this foreshadow is relationships. The Jews failed and the Christians failed, but the primary lesson from this chapter is that God never fails. His love cannot fail. Yet, what should we be doing until the prophecy of this multitude is fulfilled? What did Yeshua say? "By this all men will know that you are my disciples, if you love one another" (John 13:35). It comes down to the "golden commandment" again. We are to love God with all our hearts and love others as ourselves. It has always been about these two things, and it will always be. We will always fall short in this life, but we can always strive to do better.

Take comfort knowing the time is coming when the Messiah will return and establish His Kingdom.

Whatever situation you find yourself in right now, if love is not your driving force, it is time to become introspective. Take comfort knowing the time is coming when the Messiah will return and establish His Kingdom. In that day, life will finally be without toil again, as it was in the Garden of Eden. We will no longer strive for knowledge because we will have gained perfect wisdom. Until then, life may still require some hardship, especially in our relationships, but be wise enough to know that as an individual you must endure so that together we can attain our unity as a multitude in our promised city of gold.

PART
IV

PART
VI

CHAPTER 10

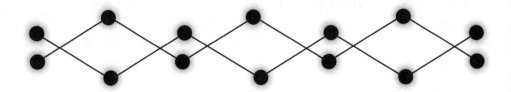

The Promised Land, Episode No. 1: God's Kingdom in Israel

"This was a real, truly live place. And I remember that some of it wasn't very nice, but most of it was beautiful... But anyway... we're home... There's really no place like home."
—Dorothy, The Wizard of Oz

Let's play a word association game. If you can, cover the answer column on the right with a book or your hand. Ready? Now, look at the first word in the left column and say or write down the first word that comes into your mind. Keep reading through the words that follow in the left column and keep saying the first word you associate with it. When you have considered the words you immediately associate with all ten words listed in the left column, check to see if you guessed correctly.

Salt and...   ...pepper
Bagels and...   ...cream cheese
Starsky and...   ...Hutch
Beauty and...   ...the Beast
Peanut butter and...   ...jelly
Laverne and...   ...Shirley
Hammer and...   ...nail
Bread and...   ...butter
Day and...   ...night
David and...   ...Goliath

How did you do? Pretty well, I'm sure. The reason we make these word associations so naturally is because they are so closely linked together in our society. As such, they instinctively flow off our lips.

Now, let me give you one more word association: The nation of Israel and_____?

The answer is "The Promised Land." Why? Because The Promised Land will always be associated with home for the Jewish people. So strong is this connection between the Jewish people and the Promised Land that when the Romans exiled the Jews in AD 70, Jews from around the world said at the end of every Passover Seder: *La Shanna Haba B'Yerushalayim*, meaning, "Next year in Jerusalem." Jews would say this in anticipation of their return to their homeland as soon as possible. Every Jewish wedding ceremony still ends today with the bridegroom breaking a glass under the heel of his shoe, originally instituted as a reminder that the Temple in Jerusalem has been destroyed and needs to be rebuilt. And one of the prayers read on every Shabbat and every Jewish Feast goes as follows: "Father of mercies, do good in Your favor unto Zion, build the walls of Jerusalem, for in You alone do we trust oh King, high and exalted God, Lord of the universe."

Even in the Book of Psalms, the psalmist cries out on behalf of the Jewish people who were living in exile in Babylon, saying:

> *"By the rivers of Babylon we sat and wept when we remembered Zion [Zion is in Jerusalem, where the Temple is.] There on the poplars we hung our harps, for there our captors asked us for songs, our tormentors demanded songs of joy; they said, 'Sing us one of the songs of Zion!' How can we sing the songs of the LORD while in a foreign land? If I forget you, O Jerusalem, may my right hand forget its skill. May my tongue cling to the roof of my mouth if I do not remember you, if I do not consider Jerusalem my highest joy"* (Psa. 137:1-6).

Considering the history linking the nation of Israel to the Promised Land, there is no way to separate the two, even though much of today's world promotes this notion. The reason the Jews and the land are forever linked are because of the everlasting Covenant promise God made to the Jewish people. This link leaves the Jewish people with a deep and incessant longing to live in the peace and security of their promised home. This chapter will explain that just as the Jewish people and the Promised Land are forever linked together in God's story, Jerusalem is yet another foreshadow of how God placed a longing in all of us to live in the peace and security of our eternal home, New Jerusalem. Ultimately, isn't life just a journey to take us back home?

In a Psalm, King David said it this way: *Sha-alu Shalom Y'rushalayim...*

> *"Pray for the peace of Jerusalem: 'May those who love you be secure. May there be peace within your walls*

and security within your citadels"' (Psa. 122:6-7).

This prayer has such a profound meaning for the Jewish people, yet it seems as if it has never been answered. The Hebrew word *Yerushalayim* means, "The City of Peace." And yet, throughout its long history, this city has been anything but a city of peace. One day, however, God will answer this prayer. And when He does, not only will Jerusalem experience peace and security forevermore, but so will the whole world. This is why we should always have our eyes fixed on what's happening to the nation of Israel and the Promised Land. When we keep our eyes fixed on these two things we know where we are in God's story.

It is a home designed by God to be a place of peace and security.

The best way of recognizing where you are in this bemusing story that God wrote is to know where the Jews are and what point on the world spectrum they currently occupy in relation to God's trilogy. They are headed back to their homeland—the Promised Land, a foreshadow about a family home for the nation of Israel. It is a home designed by God to be a place of peace and security. Unfortunately, many of us grew up in homes or still live in homes wherein—like Jews in the city of Jerusalem—we experience anything but peace and security. Some of us live in homes where we experience abuse, addiction, mental illness, or severe behavioral problems. Many people do not even have a home to live in. Others experience the unsettling emotion of having their family moved frequently and thus never have a feeling at peace or security in a home.

Abraham, the father of the nation, was originally a nomad, wandering from place to place never putting down roots. He had no place to call his home, but when God chose to make a covenant with Abraham, He promised two things: *I'm going to give you a really big family, and I'm going to give you a family home for your really big family.* When God's promises had been partially fulfilled, Abraham and his family were able to put down roots in their new family home. Today we are seeing God complete His promises to Israel with regard to them having a permanent family home. The Promised Land foreshadow is about God's plan to give all the nations a permanent, everlasting home—a home that will be peaceful and secure forever. It's about putting down eternal roots. But those roots won't be permanent until we reach the third episode, the final chapter of God's story. Until then, what should our prayer be? *La Shanna Haba B'Yerushalayim...* "Next year in Jerusalem." This should be our fervent prayer as we wait in faith, expectant and knowing God will establish our eternal home.

The Promised Land is ultimately intended to be a beautiful theocracy, and like all the other foreshadows this book explores, it unfolds in three progressive episodes: episode one is the prophetic picture of God's Kingdom in Israel, episode two is the spiritual fulfillment of God's Kingdom in us, and episode three is the eternal completion of God's Kingdom in New Jerusalem. Let's have a deeper look at how the Promised Land foreshadow progresses through the episodes.

We will begin by looking at the prophetic picture of God's kingdom in Israel. In Leviticus God said to the nation of Israel, "Follow my decrees and be careful to obey my laws, and you will live safely in the land" (Lev. 25:18). God chose this remarkably specific group of people to live in a singularly specific region of the world so they could live according to the principles of a theocracy. God would reign as their invisible King and the Israelites would be His visible subjects. It's worth noting that a subject is someone who subjects or submits themselves to someone else's authority. This theocracy was therefore intended to be an Earthly kingdom of God. It was to be a place where God's will would be done on Earth as it is done in Heaven. How is God's will done in Heaven? In Heaven, God's will is done perfectly every time.

Everyone in Heaven obeys God perfectly every time! The result of their perfect obedience means no one ever goes to bed hungry, everyone always has a roof over their head, no one is ever molested, abused or abandoned, and everyone is always treated respectfully, fairly, and equally. In Heaven, justice reigns supreme!

Yes, the Promised Land was meant to be a radical type of kingdom. It was to be a peaceful and secure home for everyone who lived within its boundaries. For this to happen the Israelites had to keep all the commandments of the Torah. The 613 instructions embedded in the Torah created a blueprint for how to love God and love others in remarkably radical ways. Sadly, this didn't happen because the Israelites were imperfect humans, as all humans are. Instead of being a peaceful and secure family home where God's will was done on Earth as it is in Heaven, it became a place of ego, selfishness, and unrest. As a consequence of Israel's failure to obey God's commandments, He allowed the Babylonians to conquer the Promised Land, and to carry off most of its inhabitants to Babylon. From the time of the Babylonian occupation in the seventh century BC, the nation of Israel was no longer in control of the Promised Land, and it would be occupied by a long list of foreign nations for the next 2,600 years. This resulted in the family home becoming a very unstable and unsafe place to live.

At about the time of the Babylonian occupation and exile, God began to speak through the prophets concerning a distant time at the end of God's story. God promised Israel He would do something to resolve these problems of instability and lack of safety by establishing an everlasting kingdom through the reign of *Maschiach*. This "Shylvester Shalom" type of warrior would defeat Israel's enemies once and for all. He would re-establish the kingdom of God in the Promised Land and this time it would be a peaceful and secure home for evermore.

Have a look at just one of these many prophetic passages from Isaiah:

"A shoot will come up from the stump of Jesse; from his roots a Branch will bear fruit... [both Jews and Christians agree this is speaking about the promised Messiah of Israel] but with righteousness he will judge the needy, with justice he will give decisions for the poor of the earth... [He will champion those who are needy and poor]

The wolf will live with the lamb, the leopard will lie down with the goat, the calf and the lion and the yearling together; and a little child will lead them. The cow will feed with the bear, their young will lie down together, and the lion will eat straw like the ox. The infant will play near the hole of the cobra, and the young child put his hand into the viper's nest. They will neither harm nor destroy on all my holy mountain, for the earth will be full of the knowledge of the LORD as the waters cover the sea In that day the Root of Jesse will stand as a banner for the peoples [a banner has always been a gathering place for the armies]; the nations will rally to him, and his place of rest will be glorious" (Isa. 11:1, 4,6-10).

In this passage we see the Messiah will not establish His eternal kingdom until the third and final episode of God's trilogy. When He does, every creature on Earth will live in peace and harmony with each other forevermore. So, for all you carnivores, unfortunately it looks like there will be no In-N-Out Burgers available in the third episode. While it might seem like a loss for some of us at this stage, it is excellent news for the animal kingdom.

Other prophetic passages from around that time mention how, in the last days, swords will be beaten into plowshares, and how we will all live in peace with each other (See Isaiah 2:4). It will be a time of everlasting peace and security, and most of the religious Jewish world throughout the ages has been anticipating the arrival of this Jewish Rambo-Messiah ever since. Most of these religious Jewish observers missed the other prophetic passages, where the same prophets in episode one foretold Messiah would first come not as a warrior-Messiah but as a suffering Messiah, to atone for the sins of humanity.

Isaiah 53 gives us the clearest prophetic text on the first coming of the Messiah:

> *"Surely He [the Messiah] took up our infirmities and carried our sorrows, yet we considered him stricken by God, smitten by him, and afflicted. But he was pierced for our transgressions, he was crushed for our iniquities; the punishment that brought us peace was upon him, and by his wounds we are healed. We all like sheep, have gone astray, each of us has turned to his own way [we all have egos, we're all selfish] and the LORD has laid on him [the Messiah] the iniquity of us all"* (Isa. 53:4-6).

As dramatic as it is, the concept of a suffering Messiah is undoubtedly clear from this passage. Yet somehow, the Jewish people throughout the ages did not recognize the suffering Messiah in these prophetic passages. Nor did they see Him in several other well-documented passages in the Hebrew prophetic scriptures These scriptures make clear references to a suffering Messiah long before the death and resurrection of Messiah Yeshua occurred in history.

Let's change gears and step back to the first Jewish exile, the Babylonian occupation of The Promised Land followed by a Persian occupation. Following the Persians came the Greek occupation, and following the Greeks, came the Romans, who crushed the Jews with an iron fist. The Roman occupation was so harsh that many Jews believed the time was ripe for their warrior-Messiah to arrive. They believed He would purge the Romans from their Promised Land and restore God's kingdom in Israel.

When Jesus began His ministry it seemed as if "Messianic fever" had swamped the Promised Land with many claiming to be the promised Messiah during the Roman occupation. One of these claimants was a Rabbi named Yeshua, who was so convincing that his Jewish followers fully believed he would restore God's kingdom in Israel. Many left everything they cherished just to follow Him. But when he talked about suffering and dying, his closest followers displayed grave concern. The headstrong Peter took Yeshua aside and initiated a rather frank Israeli conversation with Him. The story is recorded in Matthew's gospel.

Peter rebuked Jesus as though he were talking to a *meshuggana* (Yiddish for a crazy person), essentially saying to him, "You don't know how the story goes!" (paraphrase of Matt. 16:22).

Jesus, of course, gave it right back to Peter: "No Peter, you're the one who doesn't know how the story goes!" (paraphrase of Matt. 16:23).

History records the one who truly knew how the story would end.

Yet even after Jesus had suffered, died, and risen from the dead, the disciples were still caught up on their concept of a rebel-Messiah. When He appeared to them, they asked again: "Okay, Lord, now that we have this suffering and dying business out of the way, is this the time for You to finally restore the kingdom to Israel?" (Acts 1:6). At this juncture I can picture Jesus rolling His eyes, thinking, *You guys sound like a broken record.*

But here's the truth: someday Yeshua *will* return as a warrior-Messiah and he will right every wrong. Remember Dorothy's statement about the Land of Oz: "...some of it wasn't very nice, but most of it was beautiful..." We fervently look forward to Jesus righting every wrong and establishing an everlasting kingdom, but we know this will only happen when we reach the third and final chapter in God's story.

CHAPTER 11

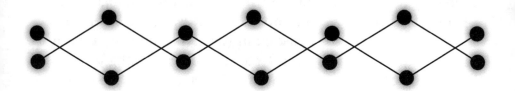

The Promised Land, Episode No. 2: God's Kingdom in Us

During the three years Rabbi Yeshua was with His disciples He taught frequently about the kingdom of God. We find numerous passages in the gospels where Jesus used phrases such as "the kingdom of God" or "the kingdom of Heaven." This concept was at the forefront of Jewish thinking and one particular instance of this thinking is referenced in Luke's gospel. A Jewish leader approached Jesus and asked when the kingdom of God would finally come as the Jews were desperate to be liberated from Roman occupation. Jesus said, "...The kingdom of God does not come with your careful observation [you can't see it], nor will people say, 'Here it is,' or 'There it is,' because the kingdom of God is within you'" (Luke 17:20-21).

This statement must surely have turned some heads. Many citizens of the Promised Land did not allow God to rule and reign in their lives, which resulted in the kingdom of God lacking power in Israel. God never forces His will on anyone and as a result, He can only rule and reign in those individuals who willingly invite Him to be their King. While every Israelite was a citizen of God's kingdom in Israel, this didn't necessarily mean God was Lord and King of every citizen's life. Unfortunately, many people, especially religious leaders, lived for their own selfish gain. Many had no true love for God and did not love others in the radical way God expected. It was in this sense that Jesus meant they could not see the kingdom of God, because the real kingdom of God is not external; it is internal. The real kingdom of God is not a specific geographical location, nor is it composed of the people who live in any one geographic location.

God never forces His will on anyone.

It is *vitally* important to understand that the kingdom of God lives only inside a human heart that is open and willing to let God rule and reign over it.

During the second episode of God's story, the soil of the Promised Land becomes the very soil of our hearts. When Jesus told the parable of the Sower, He mentioned four different types of soil—the hard soil along the path, the rocky places with shallow soil, the thorn-infested soil, and the good soil. Jesus ended this parable by saying:

> "But the one who received the seed [which is the word of God] that fell on good soil is the man who hears the word and understands it. He produces a crop, yielding a hundred, sixty or thirty times what was sown" (Matt. 13:23).

The good soil Jesus referred to is a human heart that is wide open. It is a soft heart willing to let God rule and reign over it. This kind of heart blesses and flourishes, nourishing everyone regardless of circumstance.

In another reference to the spiritual aspect of God's Kingdom, Jesus also declared, "...I tell you the truth, no one can see the kingdom of God unless he is born again" (John 3:3). To be born again means to be reborn of God's Spirit—to become a member of the family of God through faith in Messiah Yeshua.

The kingdom of God isn't an Earthly citizenship. It's a Heavenly citizenship. The kingdom of God does not comprise the citizens of Israel, nor does it comprise the citizens of America, nor the citizens of any other country. The kingdom of God is only made up of those who are born again, those who have become citizens of Heaven through faith in Messiah Jesus, and now have willing hearts to subject themselves to God's rule and reign. We become God's subjects as He becomes our worthy King.

Jesus made it simple for us by saying, "If you love me, you will obey what I command" (John 14:15). Jesus was very clear about the one basic command He gave to us: "My command is this: Love each other as I have loved you" (John 15:12).

How did Jesus love us? "Greater love has no one than this, that he lay down his life for his friends" (John 15:13). Jesus humbled Himself exchanging the glory of Heaven to suffer and die on our

> The kingdom of God lives only inside a human heart that is open and willing to let God rule and reign over it.

behalf. All He asks for in return is for us to love Him and others without reservation, the way He first loved us. This is the beauty of God's kingdom abiding in us—knowing He will never ask us to do something He has not already done. His is not a kingdom where the king sits around all day giving orders to his subjects to prevent Himself from having to do any work. In God's kingdom, the King leads by example, having first fulfilled any task expected of His subjects. A verse from Romans illustrates this important detail: "But God demonstrates his own love for us in this: While we were still sinners [while we were still cheating on Him], Christ [Messiah] died for us" (Rom. 5:8).

The fact King Jesus leads the way by example is reiterated in 1 John, which explains why we should love: "We love because he *first* loved us" (1 John 4:19). We willingly do God's will on Earth right now as it is in Heaven because God willingly laid down His life for us 2,000 years ago—even though it's still not a perfected Promised Land as of yet. It is made up entirely of people from the beginning of God's story until this present day who, through faith, have willingly opened their hearts to God's Kingship. These people are no longer citizens of Earth; they are citizens of Heaven. Earth is no longer their home because Heaven is their forever home.

CHAPTER 12

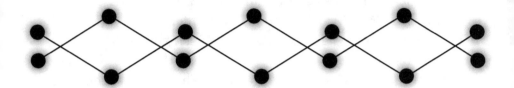

The Promised Land, Episode No. 3: God's Kingdom in New Jerusalem

A s I will remind, the best journeys always lead back home. In this third and final episode of the Promised Land, we move from God's Kingdom in us, to God's kingdom in New Jerusalem. It is in this concluding episode when we finally witness the arrival of the Jewish Rambo-Messiah, as described by many of the Jewish prophets. Revelation describes the Messiah riding on a white horse, followed by the armies of Heaven, with a sharp sword coming out of His mouth to defeat the wicked villain and his cohorts (paraphrase of Rev. 19:11-15). This is no surprise, of course, as this is the climax of God's story, where Yeshua, our Hero, comes to save the day. And what a fitting climax it is with plenty of high-tech action and drama occurring in the final scene.

The Messiah's mission in this final episode is to rid the world of injustice and evil and to establish the long-desired peaceful, secure, and everlasting home for us. Revelation describes a foolish war being waged against the Lamb, but in the end He triumphs. Scripture tells us: "...because he is Lord of lords and King of kings..." (Rev. 17:14). This story was written before time began and the irreversible outcome has always been known. There is no way to lose this war!

And with the Messiah are the elect—those who throughout history have lived by faith and willingly allowed God to rule and reign in their hearts. Revelation gives us a sneak peek at how this peaceful and secure eternal home looks:

> *"Then I saw a new heaven and a new earth, for the first heaven and the first earth had passed away, and there was no longer any sea. I saw the Holy City, the new Jerusalem, coming down out of heaven from God [Heaven and Earth merge together], prepared as a bride beautifully dressed for her husband [note the marriage language and reference to the Bride—this is the wedding]. And I heard a loud voice from the throne saying, 'Now the dwelling of God is with men, and he will live with them [the Chuppa has come down to Earth]. They will be his people, and God himself will be with them and be their God [that breathtaking moment when the Bridegroom returns for His Bride]. He will wipe every tear from their eyes. There will be no more death or mourning or crying or pain, for the old order of things has passed away'" (Rev. 21:1-4).*

No more tears. No more sadness. No more death or mourning. And something I greatly look forward to, no more pain because "...the old order of things has passed away."

Having returned from his journey, he had learned there is no place quite like home. Alas we see that, too, in the story of the prodigal son. Leaving the safety and security of his home, the prodigal son went on a journey to look for a better life. But the prodigal son's ideas did not work out well for him. Having returned from his journey, he had learned there is no place quite like home. Similarly, we are all on this crazy journey called life. In some ways we are all like the prodigal son. We are all desperately searching for a better life. We all have ideas we hope will lead us to live a better life. We have the privilege though, of knowing in advance, that the best journeys always lead back home.

In some ways we are all like the prodigal son.

Hebrews 11 talks about many heroes of faith from the past including people who, while living on this planet, lived by faith. They trusted God would keep all His promises to them. These people were still living by faith when they died and not one of them received the promises they had bet their entire lives on. And yet, they died believing God would still deliver them. These are the details described in Hebrews 11:13, which goes on to say:

> *"People who say such things show that they are looking for a country of their own. If they had been thinking of the country they had left, they would have had opportunity to return. Instead, they were longing for a better country—a heavenly one. Therefore God is not ashamed to be called their God, for he has prepared a city for them" (Heb. 11:14-16).*

Verse 13 also tells us they were "aliens and strangers" on Earth. The Earth was not their home. The truth is, all of us who have faith in God are foreigners and strangers on Earth. We are the "not yet home" people. But it will not be long until we are living forever in the peace and security of our eternal home.

How do we know it will not be long? We know by keeping our eyes on the nation of Israel and the Promised Land. Where are the Jews today? They are headed back home. And because of this, we can assume that the final chapter is close to us. In final summary, the Promised Land foreshadow begins in episode one as a prophetic picture of God's kingdom in Israel. In episode two, it becomes the spiritual fulfillment of God's kingdom in us, and in episode three, the Promised Land foreshadow becomes the eternal completion of God's kingdom in New Jerusalem.

Now that we know we are assured of a secure, eternal, family home, what do we need next? Why, family rules, of course! Let's a take a look at the fascinating foreshadow of the Torah.

PART V

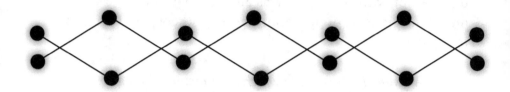

CHAPTER 13

The Torah, Episode No. 1: Rules for Imperfect Hearts

"Love rules without rules."
—Italian Proverb

D o you have any strange people in your family? Are *you* the strange person in your family? Did you say yes to both questions? Also—and this one is more painful—have you ever heard your kids telling people they have weird parents? Ouch, yes. That one stings a bit. Well next time you hear one of your children saying this, tell them to take a good look at you and your spouse because you are exactly what they will become in twenty-five years.

As relatable or humorous as some of those questions are, the truth is that it is impossible to fully understand who we are as adults, unless we first understand who we were as children. Growing up in your specific family of origin has vital consequences for who you become as an adult. Dr. Murray Bowen is one of the pioneers of the Family Systems Theory, and according to Bowen:

> *"A family is a system in which each member had a role to play and rules to respect. Members of the system are expected to respond to each other in a certain way according to their role, which is determined by relationship agreements."* [6]

I believe Dr. Bowen is suggesting that a relationship agreement is just another way of saying, "The Family Rules." Yet most of the time, families do not post these rules up on the refrigerator for everyone to see. Rather, they are learned intuitively as the members of the family interact with one other.

Consider this hypothetical example when reinforced by repetition in a child's early years of development: Dad is an alcoholic and one of the kids expresses fear when Dad breaks a few dishes in a drunken rage. Mom responds by telling the child, "Well, Dad wouldn't do that if you didn't leave your toys lying around the house." The child instantly learns something about the family rules: 1) some topics are off limits, and cannot be discussed. 2) Certain emotions cannot be displayed. 3) I can't trust my mom or dad to justly take care of me.

These points are in fact discussed by Claudia Black, Ph.D., author of *It'll Never Happen to Me*,[7] in which she suggests there are three primary rules by which every dysfunctional family lives (1). They are as follows:

---

6 Kerr, Michael E. "One Family's Story: A Primer on Bowen Theory." The Bowen Center for the Study of the Family. 2000. http://www.thebowencenter.org.
7 Black, Claudia. (1981). It'll Never Happen to Me. (Chapter 3: Children of alcoholics: As youngsters adolescents – adults. USA, A Ballantine Book: The Random House Publishing Group.

- Don't talk—some topics are off limits for discussion.

- Don't feel—some feelings are also off limits; we can laugh in this family, but don't you dare cry.

- Don't trust—the people who are meant to bring safety and comfort to me have let me down.

According to Black, when a child grows up within a dysfunctional family where these three unhealthy rules are in play, they are quick to lose their childlike innocence and will then adapt to a role in the family that will help them survive their dysfunctional childhood experience. Black lists five roles the family member is likely to adopt when growing up in a family like this. Let's have a quick look at these and while we do, think about which role you might have played in your own family.

- **The Responsible Family Hero**

  This family member adopts one of two similar mindsets: "If I don't do it no one else will!" Or, "If I don't do it, things will get worse." A family member who adopts either of these dysfunctional mindsets will often develop obsessive, perfectionist tendencies, mainly because of a driving fear of making mistakes. It is their role to do whatever it takes to save the family.

- **People Pleaser**

  Another dysfunctional family role is the Placater or People Pleaser. Their motto is: "If I am nice, I will be liked and I won't feel rejected." This personality adaptation will often drive a person to place other people's needs above their own. They struggle to set the most reasonable boundaries for people who display inappropriate behavior towards them. People who develop this type of personality aberration are often categorized as having either a codependent personality, or that of an enabler. Their motto is "peace at any price."

- **The Acting-Out Scapegoat**

  The Acting-Out Scapegoat is a role in which the family member adopts a mindset that displays inappropriate behavior: "If I make enough trouble, maybe someone will notice me!" People who adopt such a mindset usually turn out to be under-achievers, irresponsible, and sometimes self-destructive. They are often identified as the "black sheep" of the family.

- **Adjuster or Lost Child**

  The Adjuster or Lost Child is a role in which the family member adopts a mindset of withdrawal: "If I don't become emotionally involved and if I stay below the radar, I will not be hurt." People who adopt such a mindset often withdraw from the rest of the family. They often become fearful and struggle to make decisions, resulting in a lack of direction in life. This child is seeking peace and safety by trying to live in the shadows. This child is seeking peace and safety by trying to live in the shadows. They seek the safety of anonymity by attempting to go unnoticed in the family.

- **The Mascot or Jester**

  The final role is the Mascot or Jester. This family member adopts a mindset of humor or silliness in a vain attempt to take away the family pain: "If I can make people laugh, no one will have to feel any pain." People who develop this aberrant personality type usually appear to be quite immature, especially because their primary role is to distract the other family members by joking or acting silly.

Each of these adaptive roles a child may embrace in a dysfunctional family are ways to help that child survive his or her childhood. God made us extremely resilient. We have the innate capacity to adapt to almost any traumatic situation. If, however, we're still acting out any of these abnormal roles when we become adults, there are two critical factors to recognize: not only will we continue passing on our dysfunctional family system to the next generation, but we will also experience numerous problems as we attempt to live out these roles in the adult world. What worked to help us survive in our childhood doesn't work nearly so well when we become adults. Many adult children of dysfunctional families find themselves subsequently experiencing much conflict in their adult relationships.

God made us extremely resilient.

THE TORAH

The reason I explained some basics about family systems is to emphasize the importance of the Torah foreshadow which is also referred to as, "The Law." Essentially, the Torah is all about family rules and family systems. It is important to note that God handed the Torah directly to the Jewish people, through Moses, on Mount Sinai. You'll notice with all these foreshadows, God intervened directly. A quick recap reminds us the first foreshadow was the Covenant, which is a marriage. This marriage led to the birth of a family, called The Nation of Israel. This family was given a family home, called the Promised Land. We are now in a position to examine the healthy set of family rules every family needs. Knowing how a lack of healthy family rules creates chaos leading to a dysfunctional family, we can see why the Torah is important to God. It unified God's family as an individual unit and as a collective nation.

To give you an idea of the importance of the Torah in unifying God's family as a collective nation, consider their eventual return to the family home after their second exile. When the Jewish people were exiled from the Promised Land by the Romans in AD 70, they were scattered to the four corners of the Earth. Despite their separation during this exile, the Torah allowed the Jewish people to preserve their unique identity for 2,000 years. When God finally called them back home, it was as if they had never been apart. Their cultural unity was *instantaneous*. When the state of Israel was formalized in 1948, their unbroken Jewish identity immediately enabled the Israeli people to reunite as a family.

We must understand that love cannot be legislated.

As we saw in the previous chapter, just as the Jewish people cannot be separated from the Promised Land, they cannot be separated from the Torah. They are forever inseparable. As we begin our journey into the Torah, we see its ultimate purpose is to restore our imperfect human hearts. Thus, the Torah foreshadow starts out in episode one as a set of family rules written on stone tablets for governing *imperfect* hearts. It is then fulfilled by Messiah in episode two, who writes the family rules on new hearts. And finally, with perfected hearts in episode three, we will no longer have any need for written family rules. Ultimately, perfect love "rules without rules."

We must understand that love cannot be legislated. A person cannot be forced to love. To be genuine, Love must come from the heart. When we finally reach New Jerusalem in the third and final episode, we won't need any rules to govern our love because we will all live and love perfectly at all times because in God's full, glorified presence, we will not want to live or love any other way.

Until we reach this timeline in God's trilogy, we have been given rules to govern how we should love. Those rules are found in the Torah.

Now, to begin with episode one, let's examine how the Torah foreshadow begins as a set of rules given to Israel by God to govern their imperfect human hearts. Jeremiah says, "The heart is deceitful above all things and beyond cure. Who can understand it?" (Jer. 17:9). Jeremiah is pointing out the truth that we all have imperfect hearts. Our imperfect hearts are what make us human. Perfection belongs to God alone and we are not God. Some people believe we have imperfect hearts because the sin of Adam and Eve ensured every person thereafter was born with a predisposition to sin. If Adam and Eve didn't already have a predisposition to sin, why *did* they sin? If they were created as perfect human beings, why did they eat the forbidden fruit?

The reality is that Adam and Eve sinned for the same reason you and I sin today. They were not God; they were human. As Alexander Pope wisely said, "To err is human..."[8] and every human is born with an imperfect heart that leads us astray sooner or later. This has been humanity's challenge ever since God pressed the "play" button in Genesis 1:1. Imperfection is something all humans have in common.

Many generations after Adam and Eve sinned, God gave 613 family rules to the Jewish people. These rules outlined the radical ways to love God and to love others. Remember how Rabbi Yeshua explained to a certain teacher of the *Torah* how all the Law and the Prophets hang on two simple commandments? (Matt. 22:40). He was, of course, referring to these: "Love the LORD your God with all your heart and with all your soul and with all your strength" (Deut. 6:5) and, "Do not seek revenge or bear a grudge against one of your people, but love your neighbor as yourself. I am the LORD" (Lev. 19:18).

---

8 Alexander Pope, An Essay on Criticism, Part II, 1711. (The spelling of "human" as "Humane" reflects the style used in Pope's time)

Love in the Torah is always demonstrated by an action, so this radical kind of love could only happen if you obeyed the commandments. I have some Orthodox Jewish friends and if we start talking about a personal relationship with God, they will typically say, "You Jesus followers always say something like, 'I want to experience more of God. I want to go deeper with God. I want to feel you more, God!'" I'll nod and my friend will continue, "I'll tell you how we Jews experience and feel more of God. It is when we keep His commandments. We feel more of God when we obey God." This is *exactly* the kind of radical relationship God established with the nation of Israel, and there is undoubtedly merit to it.

But Jesus distilled the entire Torah—*the entire Bible, in fact*—into two basic concepts: radical ways to love God and radical ways to love others. Of the 613 Torah rules, 248 are framed in positive language, encouraging us to act in certain ways. The other 365 rules are framed in language that encourages us to refrain from behaving in certain ways. We see these rules displayed as, "Thou shall [and] …Thou shall not..." 1 John 4:8 tells us God's fundamental nature is love. This powerful truth helps us see that each of these 613 rules are merely a means of showing us *how* to love the way God loves. The way to apply the Torah in our lives today is to ask the question, "How does a 'Thou shall...' command or a 'Thou shall not...' command show us how to love God or to love others in radical ways?"

One good example of applying a Torah rule is requiring someone with a contagious infection to leave the city and stay outside until they were healed. In addition they must shout out, "...Unclean! Unclean!..." to any passersby (Lev. 13:45-46). The logical explanation for this separation is simple: if someone is contagious, the most loving thing they can do is to avoid infecting someone else. This rule makes obvious sense, whereas some other rules may not seem so straightforward. While a little more digging may be required to reveal the benefit of a specific rule, we are ultimately always able to understand how, by obeying the commandment, we are being taught to love God and love others in radical ways.

Unfortunately, the Israelites, with imperfect human hearts, failed to keep the commandments perfectly. It is crucial to recognize their failure was *not* because of a problem with the Torah as many people teach today. On the contrary, scripture unveils the goodness of God's law. King David, in reference to God, wrote: "... for your laws are good" (Psa. 119:39). The apostle Paul reiterated this, writing, "... the law is holy, and the commandment is holy, righteous and good" (Rom. 7:12).

It is essential to realize that the Torah was never the problem—the human heart was always the problem. The Israelites could not keep the Torah perfectly because their hearts were imperfect. When God prepared to exile Israel from the Promised Land the first time for failing to love God and to love others perfectly, the prophets began to speak about a time of restoration in the future. They prophesied God would replace Israel's imperfect hearts that had caused them to stumble in episode one, and He would give, not only the Jews the opportunity to receive a new spiritual heart in episode two, but all of humanity.

CHAPTER 14

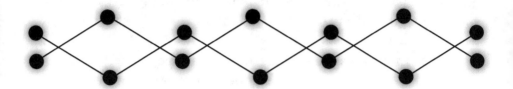

The Torah, Episode No. 2: Rules for Renewed Hearts

Episode two of the Torah is an amazing display of God's love and genius in providing a solution not only for Israel's imperfect hearts, but also the Gentile nations' hearts. The prophet, Ezekiel, foretells this phenomenon explicitly:

> *"I will give you a new heart and put a new spirit in you; I will remove from you your heart of stone and give you a heart of flesh. And I will put my Spirit in you and move you to follow my decrees and be careful to keep my laws" (Ezek. 36:26-27).*

The problem with the imperfect human heart in episode one was its reliance on human strength and human will to obey the 613 Torah commandments. In those days, God only gave His Spirit to a few select people enabling them to do extraordinary things for the kingdom of God. These select few were mainly Israel's judges and kings, like Samson, Deborah, Saul, and David. But a few of them were ordinary people, like Joseph, and Joshua. For the most part, the rest of Israel's population had to rely on their own strength and will to live the radical life God expected them to live.

What Ezekiel was describing in the passage above is a time in the then-distant future, when God would replace the imperfect, first-episode heart of humankind with a new spiritual heart. And within this new heart God's very own Holy Spirit would make His home. Joel describes who the recipients will be:

God would replace the imperfect, first-episode heart of humankind with a new spiritual heart.

"And afterward, I will pour out my Spirit on all people. Your sons and daughters will prophesy, your old men will dream dreams, your young men will see visions. Even on my servants, both men and women, I will pour out my Spirit in those days" (Joel 2:28-29).

Closer to the time of fulfillment, after Jesus died and rose from the dead, He appeared to His followers over a period of forty days, and gave them this command:

"... Do not leave Jerusalem, but wait for the gift my Father promised, which you have heard me speak about. For John baptized with water, but in a few days you will be baptized with the Holy Spirit" (Acts 1: 4-5).

The fulfillment of this event is recorded in the second chapter of Acts. During the Feast of Shavuot about one hundred and twenty followers of Rabbi Yeshua were waiting and praying in a room as commanded. The Holy Spirit fell upon the people like the sound of a mighty tempest, and what appeared to be tongues of fire rested on each person. They began to speak in a variety of languages that were completely foreign to them, but understood by the many foreign proselytes and Jewish pilgrims attending Shavuot. They heard these people babbling and due to their seemingly inebriated, yet holy behavior, some thought they were drunk.

Peter stood up and addressed the crowd, saying:

> *"... Fellow Jews and all of you who live in Jerusalem, let me explain this to you; listen carefully to what I say. These men are not drunk, as you suppose. It's only nine in the morning! No, this is what was spoken by the prophet Joel: 'In the last days,' God says, 'I will pour out my Spirit on all people...'" (Acts 2:14-17).*

Peter continued preaching that Yeshua is the promised Messiah. When he had finished, about 3,000 Jews put their faith in Messiah Jesus. From this moment in time until the present, everyone who believes in their heart and confesses with their mouth that Jesus is Lord—men and women, young and old, servants and free, Jews and Gentiles—are given God's Spirit to dwell in their hearts. We no longer have to bear the burden of loving God and others in radical ways relying exclusively on our own strength and our own will. Instead, we now have the Holy Spirit to guide us, enabling us to serve God the way He expects us to love and serve Him. We are no longer bound by rules written on tablets of stone, but we are empowered by rules written on our hearts. No longer must we function under the letter of the law, but rather under the Spirit of the law.

Now Ezekiel wasn't the only one to reference our new hearts.

The prophet, Jeremiah, clarifies this in a scripture you may recognize from a previous chapter. He references a time when God
would make a new covenant with the house of Israel and with the
house of Judah, saying,

> *"'The time is coming,' declares the LORD, 'when I will*
> *make a new covenant with the house of Israel and with*
> *the house of Judah. It will not be like the covenant I*
> *made with their forefathers when I took them by the*
> *hand to lead them out of Egypt, because they broke my*
> *covenant, though I was a husband to them,' declares*
> *the LORD. 'This is the covenant I will make with the*
> *house of Israel after that time,' declares the LORD. 'I*
> *will put my law in their minds and write it on their*
> *hearts...'" (Jer. 31:31-33).*

We obviously can see that it is still not a perfect system in episode two, but the system has been comprehensively improved,
because believers can allow the Holy Spirit to work through them,
since He lives within our hearts. This radical spiritual transformation enables believers to tap into God's heart in ways we never
could while relying entirely on our own strength and will. The result is a vast improvement empowering us to love God and people
in extraordinary new ways, just as God had planned for us from
the beginning. In fact, we now have an even broader potential for
love than the Torah ever required.

In this regard, Jesus gave us a detailed explanation concerning
the importance of the Torah, and how His life on Earth fulfilled
and expressed the beauty therein:

> *"Do not think that I have come to abolish the Law or*
> *the Prophets; I have not come to abolish them but to*
> *fulfill them. I tell you the truth, until heaven and earth*
> *disappear, not the smallest letter, not the least stroke of*

a pen, will by any means disappear from the Law until everything is accomplished" (Matt. 5:17-18).

In the passage above, Jesus is saying, "We're not done with *a written set of family rules,* at least not yet. Only when we reach episode three—when Heaven and Earth disappear—will we no longer have a need for *a written set of family rules on stone tablets or on human hearts.* Until that time, every letter and every stroke of the pen of the Torah written on your heart stands. I have come to Earth to show you how to live out the Torah in real time. I am the Living Torah."

Having explained the importance of the Torah, Jesus went on to make some distinctions between what it means to function under the letter of the law, as opposed to functioning under the Spirit of the law:

"You have heard that it was said to the people long ago, 'Do not murder, and anyone who murders will be subject to judgment.' [Yeshua is referencing one of the Ten Commandments of the Torah, stating: 'Do not murder.'] But I tell you that anyone who is angry with his brother will be subject to judgment..." (Matt. 5:21-22).

Allow me to paraphrase what Jesus is saying here: "When we start functioning under the Spirit of the law, any unresolved anger we feel towards others is literally equated to murder!" You might think, *How can this even be possible?* What Jesus means is that if you go through life without ever having murdered anyone, but at some point you develop a feeling of unresolved anger against another person, you have missed the entire point of the commandment concerning murder. Why? Because murder is very often the result of anger. Think about it; if one person really hates another it could easily devolve into murder. Murder and unresolved anger, therefore, are merely different degrees of the same heart problem.

Another distinction Yeshua made is recorded a few verses down:

> "*You have heard that it was said, 'Do not commit adultery.' But I tell you that anyone who looks at a woman lustfully has already committed adultery with her in his heart*" (Matt. 5:27-28).

In this instance, Jesus equates lustful thinking to the act of committing adultery. What He is saying is, "Even if you go through life without committing adultery, you have missed the point underlying the commandment against adultery if you still struggle with lust throughout your life." If you can do it in your heart, it can easily devolve into committing adultery. Again, adultery and lustful thoughts are merely different degrees of the same heart problem. The whole idea behind these teachings Jesus gave us is to reveal what we need to allow the Holy Spirit to work on in our lives.

When we start to understand how the Torah, in episode one, acts as a foundation for the law of the Spirit brought to us through Messiah Yeshua in episode two, we begin to realize how the requirements of the Torah haven't been lowered. They have been *raised*. With this understanding, we see how shameful the teachings are, of those who insist the Torah has been abolished. Instead, we now have the Holy Spirit in our new hearts to help us love, not by the letter, but by the Spirit of the law. This is indeed a far higher standard than the letter of the law.

One more important point before we move onto the third episode for those who might ask, "Doesn't Paul tell us in the New Testament that we are to be done with keeping the Torah?"

The answer is, "Absolutely not."

"But wouldn't Paul be in conflict with what Jesus taught about the Torah?" If you take a closer look at the verses where Paul says something seemingly negative about the Torah, you'll find that what he says we are to be done with is not about keeping the Torah, but rather about being done with teaching or believing that *salvation could be achieved by keeping the Torah* (See Acts 15:1, Romans 3:28–31, Galatians 2:15–3:7, Galatians 5:1-4). Since the beginning of time, salvation has always been and always will be a gift God gives us through the exercise of our faith. It will never be through the exercise of our works. The Torah was never intended to be our ticket to Heaven. It is our faith in God which ensures us a place in Heaven.

Again, in an astounding display of God's majesty, in episode three, the bar is raised even higher. Next, we will discover more of God's provision.

CHAPTER 15

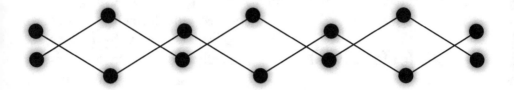

The Torah, Episode No. 3: There are No Rules for Perfect Hearts

N ow the astonishing third episode. Would you believe this standard will, in fact, rise even higher, as we move from a written set of family rules on new hearts in episode two, to no need for a written set of rules for perfected hearts in episode three? The passage in Matthew where Jesus said we will only need *written rules* until Heaven and Earth pass away is a direct reference to the third episode. When we reach that moment in the third episode, perfect love will rule without the need for us to be bound by any exterior rules. Ultimately, perfect love rules without any rules. And in this case, no rules means the standard of love gets *even higher*.

The Book of Revelation describes the perfect spiritual environment that will permeate New Jerusalem, which will be our eternal home: "Nothing impure will ever enter it, nor will anyone who does what is shameful or deceitful, but only those whose names are written in the Lamb's book of life" (Rev. 21:27). This scripture basically states that everyone in New Jerusalem will love and be loved perfectly. I'm not exactly sure how God will pull this off but my guess is that when we're finally in His full, glorious presence, and see God face to face, our response will only be to love radically and perfectly forever.

> # Our response will only be to love radically and perfectly forever.

A chapter from Paul's first letter to the Corinthian Church reinforces this awe-inspiring reality. An excerpt taken from what is commonly referred to as, "The Love Chapter" depicts the essence of this God-kind of love that we will express in New Jerusalem. To explain this better I will paraphrase 1 Corinthians 13:1–9 in my own language, but I do suggest you read the actual verses:

> *"If I speak in tongues of men and angels, but I do not have love, I'm just creating chaotic noise. If I have the gift of prophecy and I can fathom all the mysteries and knowledge, and I have faith to the point of actually being able to move mountains, but I do not have love, I am nothing! If I give all I possess to the poor and I give over my body to hardship but I do not have love, I gain nothing."*

Paul then goes on to describe what love is (verses 3–8 paraphrased; verse 8 partially included):

> *"Love is patient and kind. It does not envy, it never boasts, and it is not proud. Love does not dishonor others—in fact, it always thinks the best of others. Love*

is not self-seeking, not easily angered, and it keeps no record of wrongs—it doesn't harbor anger towards a brother. Love does not delight in evil but rejoices with the truth. It always protects, always trusts, always hopes, always perseveres. Love never fails..."

Paul continues, writing about earthly things that will come to an end (verses 8–9 paraphrased; verse 9 partially included):

"Where there are prophecies, they will cease; where there are tongues, they will be stilled; and where there is knowledge, it will pass away."

Isn't that an amazing description of the God-kind of love? And what timeframe does verse eight refer to? Paul is talking about the third episode, when Heaven and Earth pass away. Let us continue through my paraphrased version of verses eight and nine.

"For now we know in part and we prophesy in part, but when completeness comes, what is in part disappears. When I was a child I talked like a child, I thought like a child, I reasoned like a child, but when I became an adult I put childhood and childish ways behind me. Right now, all of us see only a poor reflection of God's ultimate reality, as with the reflection in a clouded mirror or looking through foggy glass; but then—when we're in the presence of God—we shall see face to face. Now I know only in part, but then everything will make sense to me. When I'm in God's presence I won't have to ask, and I won't have to call Rabbi Gene to ask a question. I won't have to see a counselor to resolve my difficult issues."

Remember, the context of this chapter is love and these verses seem to be saying that when we see God face to face, when everything makes perfect sense, then we will love and be loved perfectly.

Paul then ends this passage with an astounding statement:

> *"There are three things that will endure—faith, hope, and love—and the greatest of these is love"* (1 Cor. 13:13)

Have you ever wondered why the chapter ends this way? Why is love the greatest of these? Faith, hope, and love were all necessary in the first episode and are still needed now in the second episode. They are necessary tools to help us function optimally in our current reality. When the current Heaven and Earth disappear and New Jerusalem arrives, I believe we will no longer need faith and hope, as these are typically future-oriented tools. Faith and hope both help us to conceptualize things for which we expectantly wait: *"Now* faith is being sure of what we hope for and certain of what we do not see" (Heb. 11:1). But when the waiting is over and we finally see God face to face, I believe the only thing needed and the only thing that will remain throughout eternity is love. For this reason, love is undoubtedly the greatest of these three spiritual tools. Perfect love rules without any rules. When we are in the presence of God, seeing Him face to face (*panim al panim*) we will not need to open our Bibles to see how it is done. We will be living and experiencing it in person.

In Heaven, this perfect love will come naturally. We will experience no more disappointment, whether from the people in our lives who fall short, or through disappointment in ourselves.

There will be no more pain and no more sorrow.

Nevertheless, we are all stuck in the second episode, with many of us carrying a great deal of pain, scars, and wounds due in part to the dysfunction in our lives. Many of us have also caused others pain, scars, and wounds. I believe the Torah foreshadow is an opportunity for us to thank God for giving us His Holy Spirit, who is called "The Helper." The Holy Spirit wants to help us move closer towards more fully expressing the image of our Messiah. Our Helper wants to heal our wounds, transform our lives, and make something beautiful out of ashes. This is the loving God we serve. This is the God who wrote a story that has been progressing at a slow and steady pace. But it is a story that He has determined has a favorable ending.

How can we honestly trust everything will end well? Because we have an all-powerful Father who adores us and has promised us full access to His all-embracing love. In the next chapter, the Temple Foreshadow, we explore God's plan to remove all obstacles currently keeping us away from Him. Without these obstacles we begin to understand how we will soon live in His presence forever.

PART
VI

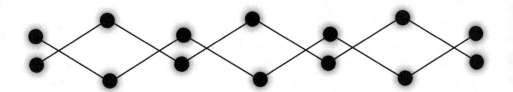

CHAPTER 16

The Temple, Episode No. 1: Distant Access to God

"The greatest gift a father can give his children is his time."
—Author unknown

M odern research shows how vital a father's presence is for the well-being of his children. Of course, this research presumes the father is emotionally healthy enough to give his children appropriate care. If statistics are anything to go by, there is no denying that when a father spends time with his children, it pays huge dividends developing the emotional and psychological health of his children.

A report published in 2006 by the U.S. Department of Health and Human services is very enlightening in this regard. This report is titled, "The Importance of Fathers in the Healthy Development of Children."[9] The following are a few relevant facts from chapter

9 Bradford, Wilcox W., Rosenberg et al. (2006). The importance of fathers in the healthy

two, titled: "Fathers and their Impact on Children's Well-Being." This chapter shows that children who have involved, caring fathers ultimately receive better educational outcomes. Fathers who are involved, nurturing, and playful give special advantages to their children, such as higher IQs and better linguistic and cognitive capacities. Fathers who exhibit these characteristics also ensure their children are more likely to feel secure, and confident exploring their surroundings. As these children grow older they are also more likely to have better social connections. They are less likely to get into trouble at home, school, or in the neighborhood. They are less likely to experience depression, to exhibit disruptive behavior, or to lie, and are more likely to exhibit pro-social behavior. Boys with involved fathers have fewer behavioral problems and girls have stronger self-esteem. Children with involved fathers are also more likely to have good physical and emotional health, to achieve academically, to avoid drugs, violence, and delinquent behaviors. The list of advantages an involved father offers his children is practically endless. These advantages form the foundation of this chapter (2).

A few years ago on a public holiday I had an interesting interaction with a man at my gym. We were in the locker room and to be friendly I said to him, "Do you have the day off?"

"Nope," he replied, "I have to work." After a short pause he added, "At least I don't have to go out of town on business this week, like I usually do, so I can finally spend some time in the evenings with my kids."

"That's great," I replied. "Kids really need to spend time with their dad."

My response triggered a strong emotional reaction in this guy. Suddenly, with great passion he began to rant about how his dad was never there for him while he was growing up. He went on to complain about how his dad had rarely been home because he traveled regularly on business trips.

development of children. Child Abuse and Neglect User Manual Series, pages 11, 12, 13. Retrieved from https://www.childwelfare.gov/pubPDFs/fatherhood.pdf 2.

"Even when my dad was home," he added, "he wasn't really home because he was in his office working. He just wasn't accessible. He was a distant father." This man became increasingly upset as he continued talking. The more distressed he became, the louder he spoke. Eventually, everyone in the locker room turned their heads to see what the heck was going on. It was a little awkward, to say the least.

At the height of his rant, I broke the tension by gently saying, "Dude! You have some serious father issues." I then handed him my business card. "Why don't you come by the church sometime to talk about it?" He took me up on my offer. We met several times, and he made some really good progress dealing with his issues. Praise the Lord.

So, how about you? Did you have a good relationship with your dad while growing up? Did he spend enough time with you? Did he make you a high priority in his life? I believe the greatest gift a father can give his children is his time. Are you perhaps still wrestling with the emotional and psychological consequences of growing up with an absentee or even a distant father? If so, I'll bet these consequences are still affecting the quality of your life today in some way.

Raising healthy kids requires a dad to spend plenty of time with his children. This ensures children have easy access to their dad, and gaining easy access to our heavenly Dad is what the Temple Foreshadow is all about.

The Temple Foreshadow begins in episode one as a prophetic picture of *distant access* to God in the old neighborhood. In episode two, it becomes spiritually fulfilled through *confident access* to God in the new neighborhood, and it is eternally completed in the final episode as *full access* to God in the perfect neighborhood.

I have had the privilege of being able to spend a lot of time in Israel. My wife and I really enjoy people watching. We especially love to watch Israelis interacting with their kids. Israel is a family-oriented society where they enjoy taking their children to just about any and every social function they attend. Israeli children, while waiting patiently for their parents to finish socializing, will often drift away from their parents to play in their imaginary world of mystery and adventure.

When a child realizes they have drifted too far from their parents, he or she will often cry out in fear, "*Abba! Abba! Eiffo atah?*" Which is Hebrew for, "Daddy! Daddy! Where are you?" When the father hears his child's cries for help, he of course rushes from wherever he is to rescue his child, swooping the child up into his arms, and life is good again.

As believers, we know we are God's children. Like all children, we have a tendency to drift too far from our Heavenly *Abba*, our Heavenly Daddy. The Temple Foreshadow is the story of God's plan to remove all the obstacles keeping us away from Him, so we can be in His presence forever.

Let's first look at how the Temple Foreshadow begins in episode one as a prophetic picture of distant access to God in the old neighborhood. Access to God was distant in ancient Israel because the Israelites had to keep themselves at a safe distance from God's powerfully holy presence.

In Exodus 25:8-9, God said to Moses:

> "*Then have them make a sanctuary for me, and I will dwell among them. Make this tabernacle and all its furnishings exactly like the pattern I will show you.*"

Based on God's instructions, the tabernacle was a portable tent-like structure erected by the Israelites every time they stopped to set up camp during their forty-year journey through the wilderness. We begin to understand the beauty of this prophetic picture and the purpose of the tabernacle when we delve into the meaning of some of the words God uses in this passage. We are about to take a little Hebrew class here, so get ready to learn some cool, new stuff.

The Hebrew word for "sanctuary" in the passage above is *mikdash*, which means a "holy place." The Hebrew word for "holy" is *kadosh*. Take note of how these two words are related: mikdash (holy place); kadosh (holy.) They sound similar because they are both built on the same three-letter root: קדש which from right to left is pronounced *QUF DALET SHIN* [gray letters in the chart below].

God is kadosh—He is holy, set apart, and it therefore makes sense that any place God chooses to dwell would have to be mikdash—a holy place set apart for Him.

ENGLISH	HEBREW	PRONUNCIATION
Sanctuary	מִקְדָּשׁ	mikdash
Holy	קָדוֹשׁ	kadosh

Now the Hebrew word in this passage for "dwell" is *shakan*, and the Hebrew word for "tabernacle" is *mishkan*. Take note of how similar these two words sound, due to them being related: shakan (dwell); mishkan (tabernacle). They sound similar because they, too are built on the same three-letter root: שכן which from right to left is pronounced *SHIN QAF NUN* [Gray letters in chart below]. We see then, God shakan (God dwells) in His mishkan (literally dwelling place). What's the point of understanding these root letters? They show us nothing less than what God ultimately wants to achieve and that is to create an exceedingly special kind of neighborhood.

Probing even deeper into the Hebrew language, we discover the Hebrew word for "neighbor" is *shaken*, and the word for "neighborhood" is *shkunah*. Maybe you can hear how all four of these words are all built on the three-letter root שׁכנ: shakan (to dwell); mishkan (dwelling place); shaken (neighbor); shkunah (neighborhood). They all describe things related to a neighborhood.

ENGLISH	HEBREW	PRONUNCIATION
Dwell	שׁכן	shakan
Tabernacle	משׁכן	mishkan
Neighbor	שׁכן	shaken
Neighborhood	שׁכונה	shkunah
Divine Presence	שׁכינה	shkinah

Even the Hebrew word, shkinah, used by the ancient rabbis to describe "Gods divine presence"—the very same Divine Presence that often manifested to the Israelites as a cloud by day and a pillar of fire at night—comes from this same three-letter root.

Many readers will recognize this Hebrew word by its common English pronunciation, as God's shekinah glory.

Shkinah depicts an image of the neighborhood lamp post. Every neighborhood needs a lamp post and this one was unequaled by any other.

What we can learn from the words used in this passage? We learn that God commanded Moses to build Him a holy dwelling place that would be at the center of this very special neighborhood.

The Book of Numbers gives us a pretty good snapshot of how this special neighborhood looked:

"The LORD said to Moses and Aaron: 'The Israelites

are to camp around the Tent of Meeting some distance from it, each man under his standard with the banners of his family"' (Num. 2:1-2).

The Israelites would camp around the perimeter of the Tent of Meeting, which is synonymous with the "tabernacle." Each man stood under his own standard, along with banners of his clan. Picture all twelve of the Jewish tribes and their families, probably between two to three million people in total, encamped or encircled around God's dwelling place. This was a huge group of people and a tremendously large neighborhood. To help you visualize how fascinating this special neighborhood would have been, I have included an artist's rendering of the only true theocracy ever to have existed.

Figure 1: Artist Credit: Yvette Beatrice Y. Co. Oil painting on canvas. 2012

Can you see how God dwelled at the very center of this first-episode neighborhood and the people dwelled around Him? This model was continued on a larger scale when the Israelites settled down in the Promised Land and King Solomon had built a permanent Temple in Jerusalem.

With this visual, it is easy to see now the main purpose of this special neighborhood was to provide the Israelites access to God. Even though the tabernacle was at the center of the camp in this first episode, however, it remained a distant access to God for the Israelites, first via the tabernacle and then the Temple. We take the Holy Spirit's indwelling presence for granted, but it is important to remember God is kadosh—He is holy, while the people were unholy. They were, therefore, only able to come as near to God as the outer courtyard to bring their offerings.

The courtyard leads into the first room called the Holy Place. God kept Himself at a safe distance, dwelling in the furthermost room, called the Holy of Holies, while a curtain separated the two rooms from one other. The Israelites could come into pretty close proximity with God in the courtyard with their offerings, but they could not come into direct contact with God's holy presence, or else they would die. Death was, and still is, the penalty for sin. Remember, this is why through this first-episode sacrificial system of the Temple, God accepted the blood of an animal as a substitute, as an atonement for the blood of the Israelites. Viewed in this light, the Temple can be considered as a kind of holiness-creating factory.

Leviticus says it this way: "For the life of a creature is in the blood, and I have given it to you to make atonement for yourselves on the altar; it is the blood that makes atonement for one's life" (Lev. 17:11). The Book of Hebrews expands on this concept: "In fact, the law [the Torah] requires that nearly everything be cleansed with blood, and without the shedding of blood there is no forgiveness" (Heb. 9:22).

In episode one of God's trilogy, the feast of *Yom Kippur* represented the annual pinnacle of these blood sacrifices. Yom Kippur means, "the Day of Atonement" and it was the only time of year a man could enter into the Most Holy Place. Only the high priest was able to enter, and he could do so only after a thorough, ritual cleansing. On this special day given to the Israelites to atone for their sins, they would gather around the outside of the Temple walls. The high priest would use two goats for the atonement ceremony. One of the goats would be sacrificed on the alter in the outer courtyard, and the high priest would take its blood and pass through the first room of the tent, the Holy Place. He would then pass through the safety curtain separating the Holy Place from the Holy of Holies, entering into the room where God's shekinah glory was dwelling.

The Ark of the Covenant rested inside this most Holy Place, and the lid of the Ark was called "the Mercy Seat of God." This appropriate name reflects God's mercy in spite of our human failings. The high priest would then sprinkle the blood of the goat on the Mercy Seat of God and go back out to the courtyard where he would place his hands on the second goat. This symbolic act transferred the sins of the people to the cursed goat, which would then be released into the wilderness. The sacrifice of the first goat and the sprinkling of its blood, along with the release of the second goat, enabled God to forgive the sins of the entire nation of Israel. Yom Kippur was a day of national forgiveness of sins.

People often ask how the Jewish people were saved in Old Testament days and the answer lies in the Feast of Yom Kippur, when they received atonement for their sins through the blood sacrifice of an animal. Believers are saved today through the blood sacrifice of Jesus. Both require faith to be effective. A casual observation of the Temple sacrificial system reveals that it was an insufficient system. The first reason being that after they were forgiven, the Israelites still could not stand in God's holy presence and live. This distant access is obviously not ideal between our Heavenly Father and His children because it is built on a fear of judgment. Yet, as we will see in the second episode, God was working out a plan to move to a better kind of access to Himself.

The second reason is the Jewish people had to come back year after year because they were never really free from the heavy burden of sin. For as soon as they left the Temple, they immediately began accruing spiritual debt again. The repetitive cycle of guilt and shame followed by forgiveness was never-ending. The author of Hebrews wrote extensively about the insufficiency of Yom Kippur, stating in chapter ten: "The law [the Torah] is only a shadow of the good things that are coming—not the realities themselves..." (partial rendering of Heb. 10:1).

Everything in the Torah is a foreshadow.

Everything in the Torah is a foreshadow, or prophetic picture of something God planned to fulfill later on in His story. The author of Hebrews is building up to an argument demonstrating how the feast of Yom Kippur was foreshadowing something far greater that would in fact create the seamless transition to episode two. The author of Hebrews goes on to say:

> "...For this reason it [meaning Yom Kippur] can never, by the same sacrifices repeated endlessly year after year, make perfect those who draw near to worship. If it could, would they not have stopped being offered? For the worshipers would have been cleansed once for all, and would no longer have felt guilty for their sins. But those sacrifices are an annual reminder of sins, because it is impossible for the blood of bulls and goats to take away sins" (partial rendering of Heb. 10:1 and complete rendering of 10:2-4).

This passage clearly creates an argument saying that not only was the sacrificial system insufficient, but it was intended to be temporary. The system was God's stop-gap solution to our problem of sin. The blood of sacrificed animals could never really do the job permanently because animals are a poor substitute for mankind. For a substitute to be fully sufficient it would ultimately take a much greater sacrifice than an animal—a sacrifice that would not require an annual return. It would take a sacrifice that resolved the issue of sin forever—a sacrifice absolving all of us from sin. Of course, this kind of sacrifice would be infinitely special for it required someone who was perfect, unblemished, and entirely pure (holy.) It required nothing less than the Superhero of God's spectacular story. Yes, the Mashiach, the Messiah, the Savior, the Holy One of Israel would have to willingly die at *His Father's own hand.*

Paul's second letter to the Corinthians explains this sacrifice well: "God made him [the Messiah] who had no sin to be sin for us, so that in him we might become the righteousness of God" (2 Cor. 5:21). Righteousness means to be made holy. This powerful scripture eloquently unveils that God had a plan from the very beginning to fix the insufficiency of Yom Kippur. God would move the Temple foreshadow from a distant access to God in the first episode to a *confident access to God* in the second episode, as our Heavenly Dad discovers a new neighborhood to reside in.

CHAPTER 17

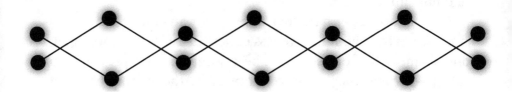

The Temple, Episode No. 2: Confident Access to God

Remember the Israeli dad who runs to his child who is crying, "Abba! Abba! Where are you?" Well, in a similar way, God ran to Earth to rescue us. Our great Superhero left the comfort of Heaven and ran to Earth to rescue His Bride. The Book of Hebrews has this to say concerning the work completed by the Messiah:

> *"When Christ (Messiah) came as high priest of the good things that are already here, he went through the greater and more perfect tabernacle that is not man-made, that is to say, not a part of this creation. He did not enter by means of the blood of goats and calves; but he entered the Most Holy Place once for all by his own blood, having obtained eternal redemption" (Heb. 9:11-12).*

What does eternal redemption mean? It means there is no need for Him to come back year after year. Our redemption is eternal and not annual.

We will no longer have to accrue sin for an entire year. We do not have to fret about forgiveness either. There is to be more guilt and shame. All of our sins have been forgiven: past, present, and future—because they're forever covered by the atoning blood of our mighty Messiah, Yeshua. The Book of Hebrews says it this way:

> *"Therefore, brothers, since we have confidence to enter the Most Holy Place by the blood of Jesus, by a new and living way opened for us through the curtain, that is, his body, and since we have a great priest over the house of God, let us draw near to God with a sincere heart in full assurance of faith, having our hearts sprinkled to cleanse us from a guilty conscience and having our bodies washed with pure water"* *(Hebrews 10:19-22).*

All of our sins have been forgiven.

We now have new confidence to boldly approach God because He currently dwells in the center of a new neighborhood—He lives in **us**.

Scripture is explicit on this matter: "Don't you know that you yourselves are God's temple and that God's Spirit lives in you?" (1 Cor. 3:16). Through faith in Yeshua, the shkinah—God's shekinah glory, His holy presence—comes to make a home inside of us. Light emanating from the neighborhood lamp post, the light of God, is in us now. Which is why Yeshua said, "You are the light of the world… and who lights a lamp and puts it under a shade?" (paraphrase of Matt. 5:14-15).

We are not the light, but the Light lives within us—the shkinah. We can now have this personal and intimate relationship with the living God. He's right here, every day, moment by moment, and if you want to, you can hang out with Him anytime without fear of judgment. There no longer is any wondering as to whether or not God will forgive you of your sins next year.

CHAPTER 18

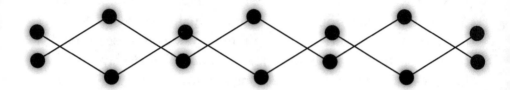

The Temple, Episode No. 3: Full Access to God

A s great as this new, *confident* access is for us who believe, God has an even better plan to move it further along. He will move it from our confident access in this new neighborhood to *full access* in a perfect neighborhood in the final chapter of His story.

The author of the Book of Revelation was given a sneak peak of our eternal home, and this is how he describes it:

> *"I saw the Holy City, the new Jerusalem, coming down out of heaven from God, prepared as a bride beautifully dressed for her husband. And I heard a loud voice from the throne saying, 'Now the dwelling [tabernacle or mishkan] of God is with men, and he will live [dwell or shakan] with them. They will be his people, and God himself will be with them and be their God'"* (Rev. 21:2-3).

God had planned to dwell in the midst of his eternal family all along! In the spirit of the late Mr. Rogers, it was *always Abba's* intention "...to have a neighbor just like you. He always wanted to live in a neighborhood with you, would you be Mine, could you be Mine, won't you be My neighbor?" It's interesting to note when the author of the Book of Revelation, in his Heavenly vision looked around this city, he saw no Temple. It makes sense for John to look for the Temple, being a Jew. Orthodox Jews today are still looking forward to the Temple being rebuilt.

Even though John looked for a Temple, he did not see one. At least, he didn't see the kind of Temple he was expecting to see. What did he see? Scripture informs us: "I did not see a temple in the city, because the Lord God Almighty and the Lamb (Jesus) are its temple" (Rev. 21:22). I have no idea what that temple looks like, but I do know it's going to be the best neighborhood you have ever lived in. And not only will God and Jesus be the Temple, but He will continue to be the Light shining from our neighborhood lamp post: "The city does not need the sun or the moon to shine on it, for the glory of God gives it light, and the Lamb is its lamp" (Rev. 21:23).

We certainly do have a good Father.

Have you ever wondered why Jesus is called the Lamb? In the Book of Revelation, especially toward the end of the book, "Lamb" is used several times. There is also a reference to "...those whose names are written in the Lamb's book of life" (Rev. 21:27). But why the Lamb?

I think this name will serve as a reminder of God's great love for us and of what He has done for us. When Thomas doubted the resurrection of Jesus, Jesus showed him His hands revealing the holes where the nails had pierced Him. He then showed Thomas His side revealing the gash where the spear had pierced Him. This was the Messiah's resurrected body—the same Messiah we will see face to face in New Jerusalem. He has holes in His hands and a hole in His side. And this, in conjunction with Him being called "the Lamb," will forevermore remind us of God's great love for us. It will be a reminder of how our Messiah, the sacrificed Lamb, ran from Heaven to Earth to rescue us and to provide a way for us to have easy, 24/7 access to our Heavenly Father. We certainly do have a good Father. He sacrificed His own son so that we could dwell in the midst of Their eternal family. It will be a perfect neighborhood.

The power of these foreshadows is expressed through the patterns they unveil. We have now been assured of having full and constant access to our loving Father in episode three of His trilogy, so we can confidently turn to the next foreshadow—the Sabbath. In this foreshadow we will learn the meaning of true rest. Some believe rest is found in being idle, but we will learn that humanity can only ever enter into true rest through God's perfect plan. In this exciting foreshadow, we will learn how to ultimately access *His rest*.

PART VII

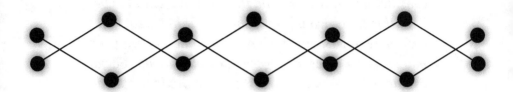

CHAPTER 19

The Sabbath, Episode No. 1: Ceasing One Day From Our Work

True rest is not being idle, it is being purposeful.

In this chapter, I want to ask you to remain focused as there is a fair amount of "technical" scriptural material to absorb. But I promise you that it leads to an exceptionally intriguing twist toward the end. Keep working through these pages and it will pay off. An article in *The Economist* said this about busyness:

> *"The predictions sounded like promises: in the future, working hours would be short and vacations long. 'Our grandchildren', reckoned John Maynard Keynes in 1930, would work around 'three hours a day'—and*

probably only by choice. Economic progress and technological advances had already shrunk working hours considerably by his day, and there was no reason to believe this trend would not continue. Whizzy cars and ever more time-saving tools and appliances guaranteed more speed and less drudgery in all parts of life. Social psychologists began to fret: whatever would people do with all their free time?" [10]

I think we can all agree that our modern world did not turn out the way Maynard Keynes predicted. In a similar vein, *New York Times* writer, Tim Kreider, says this about American busyness:

"If you live in America in the 21st century you've probably had to listen to a lot of people tell you how busy they are. It's become the default response when you ask anyone how they're doing: 'Busy!' 'So busy.' 'Crazy busy.' It is, pretty obviously, a boast disguised as a complaint. And the stock response is a kind of congratulation: 'That's a good problem to have,' or 'Better than the opposite.'

It's not as if any of us wants to live like this; it's something we collectively force one another to do.

Notice it isn't generally people pulling back-to-back shifts in the I.C.U. or commuting by bus to three minimum-wage jobs who tell you how busy they are; what those people are is not busy but tired. Exhausted. Dead on their feet. It's almost always people whose lamented

---

10 "In search of lost time. Why is everyone so busy?" The Economist. Retrieved February 17, 2017 from http://www.economist.com/news/christmas-specials/21636612-time-poverty-problem-partly-perception-and-partly-distribution-why

> *busyness is purely self-imposed: work and obligations they've taken on voluntarily, classes and activities they've 'encouraged' their kids to participate in. They're busy because of their own ambition or drive or anxiety, because they're addicted to busyness and dread what they might have to face in its absence."* [11]

If we are honest with ourselves, most of us are addicted to busyness, and the technology we hoped would make our lives easier has potentially increased the craziness of our lives. Instead of giving us more free time, the reality is, the Internet and our cell phones have dictated the path to keeping us all much busier than we'd like.

When God created the universe, He established a set number of daily hours, to which the entire world is subject. We all have twenty-four hours in a day. So, the real question is not, "Are we too busy with the twenty-four hours we're given each day?" but rather, "What are we doing with those hours?" True rest is not found in being idle, it's found in being *purposeful*. This is the essence of the message given to us in the Sabbath foreshadow.

The Sabbath is a twenty-four-hour break at the end of the week, requiring us to live differently than the other six days. If we live the Sabbath correctly we will feel refreshed and energized.

The Sabbath foreshadow began in the first episode of God's story as a prophetic picture of us ceasing our work for one day. This becomes spiritually fulfilled with us ceasing everyday from

True rest is not found in being idle, it's found in being purposeful.

11 Kreider, Tim, ANXIETY the 'busy' trap. The New York Times. Opinionator. Retrieved February 17, 2017 from https://opinionator.blogs.nytimes.com/2012/06/30/the-busy-trap

our work in episode two. The Sabbath foreshadow is eternally completed as we cease forever from our work in the third and final episode of God's story, in New Jerusalem.

One important point to remember from chapter three is that this book focuses on how each foreshadow becomes spiritually fulfilled and eternally completed, but not ever replaced. This book does not get into the details of how to observe a weekly Sabbath day of rest set apart for the Lord.

Let's begin by looking at how the Sabbath is the ceasing of our work for one day in episode one. In Deuteronomy, the fourth of the Ten Commandments says this:

> *"Observe the Sabbath day by keeping it holy, as the LORD your God has commanded you. Six days you shall labor and do all your work, but the seventh day is a Sabbath to the LORD your God..." (Deut. 5:12-14).*

Added to this, Exodus outlines the consequence of not observing the Sabbath: "...Whoever does any work on the Sabbath day must be put to death" (Exod. 31:15). The seriousness of this commandment demands our attention. In episode one, if you did not stop working on Shabbat you would die. One important message conveyed in the Sabbath foreshadow is that God makes an important connection between our work and death. Notice Shabbat is built on the pattern of creation. Over six days God created the universe, but on the seventh day, He rested. Not in the sense that He stopped doing anything, but merely in the sense He stopped the work of creating.

Now here's some interesting detail in the original meaning of the Hebrew word, Shabbat. It is much closer in English to the word "cessation" or "cease" than it is to the more commonly associated term, "rest." The word, "cease" is a better English translation than "rest" because when God stopped creating the universe,

He didn't relax on the couch to take a long nap. On the contrary, on the seventh day, God began overseeing the universe He had just created and He has been doing that ever since. In fact, Psalm 121 tells us that the God who watches over us "...will neither slumber nor sleep" (Psal. 121:4).

This is an important point to distinguish because even though part of the purpose of the Sabbath is for us to become refreshed and energized, we cannot accomplish this by taking a lazy twenty-four-hour snooze on the couch. We are to change the focus of the *type* of work we do on this day. To illustrate my point, two groupings of words found in Deuteronomy 5 hold the secret to unlocking the true purpose of the Sabbath. The first grouping found in verse thirteen contains the words, "your work." This verse explains that we are meant to do our own work for the first six days of the week and this refers to all the activities by which we manage our lives. These are our everyday activities like going to work, driving kids around, grocery shopping, and other things such as getting your hair cut.

The wording in this passage is clear and intentional, "Six days you shall labor and do all your work." The Hebrew phrase for "all your work" is *kol m'lach-techa*, which literally reads "all the work to you." All the work that belongs to you. In Jewish Sabbath-related law, the word "*kol*" means "all" so adding the word for "work," *m'lach-techa*, equates to all the activities forbidden to us on the Sabbath. *M'lach-techa* is also sometimes translated in the Bible as "business." For six days we can go about our business, or more clearly, the business that belongs to us.

The passage then goes on to say, "...but the seventh day is a Sabbath to the LORD your God." The Hebrew translation, *shabbat l'adonai*, means, "a ceasing to the Lord." Here we can see the first six days are meant to support our own kingdom, while the seventh day is reserved exclusively for supporting God's kingdom. Bear in mind, this does not mean we are not expected to support God's kingdom during the first six days of the week. However, the seventh day is an exclusive day that belongs solely to God.

The Bible doesn't explicitly list everything God considers to be our work, so just to play it safe, over time the rabbis came up with thirty-nine categories of labor they considered to be "our work" [12]. The categories are outlined as follows:

> *Carrying, burning, extinguishing, finishing, writing, erasing, cooking, washing, sewing, tearing, sifting, knotting, untying, plowing, planting, reaping, harvesting, threshing, winnowing, selecting, grinding, kneading, combing, spinning, dyeing, chain-stitching, warping, weaving, unraveling, building, demolishing, trapping, shearing, shaping, slaughtering, skinning, tanning, smoothing, and marking.*

[Sabbath- Day of Eternity by Aryeh Kaplan, p. 32]

Reading this list on the Sabbath would appear to be a violation!

Each one of these thirty-nine categories includes hundreds of sub-categories with specific rules about how to avoid crossing the line into work. There are rules about how many steps you can take before it is considered work, how much weight you can carry, how to dress, how to eat, and how to drink. Every situation imaginable is taken into account. Even today, devoutly religious Jews are careful so as to avoid violating the "no-work" rule of Shabbat.

You might think, *this is absolutely ridiculous.* When you consider it more carefully though, God made death the penalty for violating Shabbat. Understandably the Jews did their best to keep this commandment. In their well-intended zeal not to violate this no-work rule, the ancient Israelites, over time, began to lose sight

---

12 The Aryeh Kaplan Series, Copyright 1974 Aryeh Kaplan, "Sabbath-Day of Eternity" New Edition Copyright 1982, 1993 (OU/NCSY Pg. 32).

of the *spirit* of Shabbat and focused on the letter of Shabbat, produced by overprotective rabbis. They were careful to cease from doing the work *that belonged to them* on Shabbat, but they often failed to do the *work belonging to God.*

There are several examples where Yeshua addressed this error. One is found in Luke's gospel, where Jesus seemingly broke the rabbis' Sabbath rules:

> *"On a Sabbath Jesus was teaching in one of the synagogues, and a woman was there who had been crippled by a spirit for eighteen years. She was bent over and could not straighten up at all. When Jesus saw her, he called her forward and said to her, 'Woman, you are set free from your infirmity.' Then he put his hands on her, and immediately she straightened up and praised God" (Luke 13:10-13).*

Remember, Jesus was a Rabbi, a highly respected teacher. Nonetheless, the synagogue leader was not deterred from having his say:

> *"Indignant because Jesus had healed on the Sabbath, the synagogue ruler said to the people, 'There are six days for work. So come and be healed on those days, not on the Sabbath'"* (Luke 13:14).

The answer Jesus gave him puts into context the double standard the religious leaders had developed:

> *"The Lord answered him, 'You hypocrites! Doesn't each of you on the Sabbath untie his ox or donkey from the stall and lead it out to give it water? Then should not this woman, a daughter of Abraham, whom Satan has kept bound for eighteen long years, be set free on the*

Sabbath day from what bound her?"' (Luke 13:15-16).

I really love the way this story ends: "When he said this, all his opponents [meaning the religious leaders] were humiliated, but the people were delighted with all the wonderful things he was doing" (Luke 13:17).

Why were the people delighted? Because Jesus was not interested in being religiously correct. He was not impressed with false piety, especially when it interfered with loving God and loving others in a radical way.

Mark's gospel offers another example where Yeshua addressed the error of focusing on the letter of Shabbat, rather than the spirit of Shabbat. Jesus and His disciples were walking through the grain fields and his disciples were picking grain on the Sabbath, another activity forbidden by the rabbis. On this occasion, the Pharisees asked Jesus why His disciples were "...doing what is unlawful on the Sabbath?" (Mark 2:24). Jesus responded by giving them the example of David and his companions eating consecrated bread in their hour of need, and then He added:

> "...The Sabbath was made for man, not man for the Sabbath. So the Son of Man is Lord even of the Sabbath" (Mark 2:27-28).

What Jesus says here is fascinating. He is essentially saying the Sabbath was not made to imprison us, but instead to *liberate* us. It was made to set us free from the urgency of our own needs so that we can love God and others in radical ways. He was saying, "Since I am God incarnate here on Earth, I am demonstrating how to live out the Sabbath correctly." And that is exactly what He did. If we consider the scripture stating, "Through Him all things were made; without Him nothing was made that has been made," it makes good sense Jesus knows why the Sabbath was created (John 1:3).

This rabbinical error originated because death was the consequence for violating Shabbat. Why would God give such a heavy penalty concerning the Sabbath, though? Is this not perhaps an extreme consequence simply for doing some work you're not supposed to do? After all, it is not as if God was punishing someone for murder, rape, or theft. The answer to this question is found in the first half of Deuteronomy 5:12: "Observe the Sabbath day *by keeping it holy...*" Keeping the Sabbath holy is clearly the important detail. We know, having examined the Temple foreshadow, we are all imperfect and therefore unholy, and whenever something unholy meets something holy, death occurs.

God made the Sabbath holy, and because we are all unholy, the question is, how do we become holy on the Sabbath to avoid death? The answer is both simple and beautiful—*we cease from doing all the work that belongs to us.* Within the context of the Sabbath foreshadow, if we put our faith in our own work, we will die. If we put our faith in God's work, we will live. It really is that simple. This is a familiar message to believers as it is the essence of the gospel message: If we put our faith in God's work (the work done by Yeshua on the cross) we will live. Isn't that just amazing? Thank God for Yeshua, who came to set the perfect example.

> # The Sabbath was not made to imprison us, but instead to liberate us.

We have now seen the Sabbath begin as a prophetic picture of ceasing for one day from all of our work in episode one. Now, let's explore how it becomes spiritually fulfilled in episode two by ceasing everyday from all of our work.

CHAPTER 20

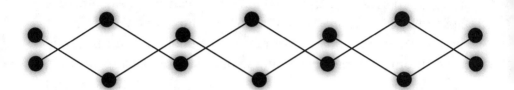

The Sabbath, Episode No. 2: Ceasing Everyday From Our Work

This is where it really starts to get good. Remember, Jesus came to liberate us from the letter of the Sabbath. Now, getting back to ceasing from our own work, predictably, the bar is raised even higher in episode two. Ephesians tells us the only way to be saved is to stop relying on our works:

> *"For it is by grace you have been saved, through faith— and this not from yourselves, it is the gift of God— not by works, so that no one can boast. For we are God's workmanship, created in Christ Jesus [Messiah Yeshua] to do good works, which God prepared in advance for us to do" (Eph. 2:8-10).*

Paraphrased, this passage explains that if we cease from doing all our work, we will be saved and will not experience spiritual death, which was the foreshadow of violating the rest of God in the first episode This is a crucial detail because it means there is absolutely no activity we can do to save ourselves. We can never be good enough and we can never give enough. We can spend every moment of our lives going to our place of worship, praying, and reading the Bible, yet we still have no chance of saving ourselves.

The only way to be saved (in this context, to be made holy) is to stop relying on our works. The only way to be saved is to rely solely on the work God did for us to atone for our sins with His own blood. It is by grace we are saved. It is not by our works, but through our belief Yeshua has already done the work for us on the cross.

Now, similar to the episode one foreshadow, it is important to note we do not cease our works just so we can take a long nap on the couch. When we have secured a place in eternity we are not given a license to snooze until Jesus comes back.

In episode two, we cease everyday from our works (instead of one day), so we can focus on God's work. This is why Ephesians 2:10 says: "For we are God's workmanship, created in Christ Jesus [Messiah Yeshua] to do good works, which God prepared in advance for us to do." In other words, through faith we are now liberated to start loving God and others in radical ways. We see in this scripture God's master plan unfolding as this is something He

> It is not by our works, but through our belief Yeshua has already done the work for us on the cross.

planned for us before the creation of the universe. Doing *His good works* was always part of God's intent for us.

In John's gospel, Jesus explains eloquently the futility of relying on our own works when He supernaturally fed a hungry crowd of at least 5,000 people (See John 6:9-13). Jesus produced enough food for the crowd from five small barley loaves and two small fish. Some of the people there were so impressed they followed Him to His next destination. Appearing to bump into Him again by chance, they asked him, "Oh, Rabbi Yeshua, when did you get here?" (paraphrase of John 6:25). With a small stretch of imagination, you can probably picture Yeshua shaking His head and saying, *"Oy vey, oy, oy, vey!"*

His recorded response was, "...I tell you the truth, you are looking for me, not because you saw miraculous signs but because you ate the loaves and had your fill (and perhaps you'd like another free meal?)" (John 6:26—my addition in parentheses). But what Jesus said next is important: "Do not work for food that spoils, but for food that endures to eternal life, which the Son of Man will give you..." (John 6:27).

Jesus was directly referencing how God sent the Israelites a free meal in the form of manna—a bread-like substance—every day while they wandered the desert for forty years (recorded in Exodus 16). God rained down manna from Heaven six days a week for forty years, but there was one important condition attached to this free meal: the Israelites could gather as much as they wanted, but whatever they gathered had to be eaten by the end of that same day. Any manna they tried to keep overnight would rot and become infested with maggots by the next morning. The only exception was the day before Shabbat. On the sixth day, they could gather a double portion and keep it overnight, without the manna rotting. This was so they did not have to work the next day, which was the Sabbath day.

Now here's the crazy part. Even though the people knew the manna would rot every time if they stored an extra portion overnight, some still collected more than they needed. Of course, this produced the same result every time. The manna would rot. "Do not work for food that spoils," Jesus advised the people who followed Him.

Doesn't it seem ridiculously exhausting to go out and work every day for something you know is just going to rot? Doesn't this strike you as absolutely crazy? Have you made the "a-ha" connection yet? Isn't this what most of us do each and every day of our lives? We go out into the world, work ourselves to exhaustion, stagger home, then we rise early to go out and do it all over again the next day. And the next day. And the next. Yet, the same principle applies—most of what we work so hard to collect each day will only rot in the end.

Most of us leave our homes each day to work for things that are only going to rot.

The principle lesson of the manna is this: excess manna the Israelites worked to collect is referred to in the Bible as *unbelief.* Their unbelief showed they didn't trust God would come through for them the next day. Even though He had provided for them day after day, *for forty years,* they still struggled to believe He would provide again the next day. It is such a strange mindset. It is as if they thought, *Okay, Lord, so You have faithfully provided for us for thirty-nine years now, but what about tomorrow?* They took matters into their own hands, doing their own works. As strange as this mindset may seem, most modern believers are still locked into this pattern of unbelief. Most of us leave our homes each day to work for things that are only going to rot.

Those Israelites who collected just enough manna for that day are referred to in the Bible as having *faith*. Their obedience revealed their trust in God. They ceased from doing their own work, and left it in God's hands. "Do not work for food that spoils, but for food that endures to eternal life..."

When Jesus spoke these words the crowd responded, "What must we do to do the works God requires?" (John 6:28).

Jesus answered, "The work of God is this: to believe in the one he has sent" (partial rendition of John 6:29). This is powerful. We see here that *faith* is ultimately the spiritual fulfillment of Shabbat. This faith in God trusts He will provide for our daily needs, but more importantly, faith in God for providing eternal, spiritual nourishment in the form of Messiah Yeshua.

The Israelites became holy by ceasing from their work for an entire day and focusing solely on God's work during the Sabbath. As such, they avoided spiritual death. Now, we in the second episode, become holy by ceasing from our works *for an entire lifetime*. When we trust and rely on the work God has already done for us, we avoid spiritual death. This is God's gift to us. His great love for us ensures we have been saved by His divine grace through our faith, and not by our works.

God not only planned to save us through our faith, He also planned for us to do good works produced by our faith. Trusting in our own works will never produce our salvation, but our new faith should produce the good works God planned for us before the beginning of time. The connection then, between Shabbat in the first episode, and the path to our salvation in the second episode, is purely and simply ceasing from our own works and placing our *faith solely in God's work.*

We move now to the third episode of the Sabbath foreshadow. Despite the vast improvement we currently experience through Messiah's intervention in God's story, the Sabbath foreshadow moves from ceasing everyday from all our works in the second episode, to ceasing forever from all of our works in episode three.

CHAPTER 21

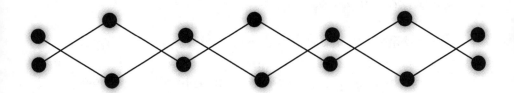

The Sabbath, Episode No. 3: Ceasing Forever From Our Work

Are you ready to get excited in the third episode? The Book of Revelation says this about New Jerusalem:

"No longer will there be any curse. The throne of God and of the Lamb will be in the city, and his servants will serve him" (Rev. 22:3).

What curse is being referenced? It is the curse keeping you and me toiling in our work. After Adam and Eve sinned, God said to Adam:

"... Cursed is the ground because of you; through painful toil you will eat of it all the days of your life. It will produce thorns and thistles for you, and you will eat

the plants of the field. By the sweat of your brow you will eat your food until you return to the ground..." (Genesis 3:17-19).

Since that curse in Genesis 3, people have been *toiling*. This is why we give our work such unflattering names, like daily slog, drudgery, the daily grind, or the coalmine. In New Jerusalem, we will no longer be working by the sweat of our brow because the curse will be removed forever. For all eternity we will no longer be doing our own work, but God's work. We will be serving Him, we will be working effortlessly to accomplish His divine will, and we will be worshiping our King. That truly sounds like paradise to me.

> **Because real rest is not about being idle, it's about being purposeful.**

Now let me show you a very interesting point about the single Hebrew word for "work" and "worship." In Hebrew these two words are exactly the same: *avodah*. When renewing His covenant with Moses and the Israelites on Mount Sinai, God said, "Six days you shall labor [avodah], but on the seventh day you shall rest [shabbat]..." (Exod. 34:21). Before the Israelites had left Egypt, the Lord told Moses to go to Pharaoh and say to him, "...This is what the LORD says: 'Let my people go, so that they may worship [avodah] me'" (Exod. 8:1).

In Hebrew there is no separation between secular and sacred, especially when it comes to work. It has always been God's plan to integrate work and worship, and He finally accomplishes this in eternity. Have you ever asked yourself what we will be doing for all eternity? Will it be one long, eternal, lazy nap on the couch?

No, we will finally love God and love others in the radical ways God intended. The beauty of our eternal work and worship is that we will never become weary of serving God in this way.

How can that be? Because real rest is not about being idle, it's about being purposeful. Perhaps you feel overwhelmed and weary with life? Perhaps you feel it has become too much just to keep your boat afloat every day. Generally, when people start out in life, they lean their ladder against a particular wall, thinking it will take them up to a satisfying and successful place. Yet most of us climb and climb, doggedly reaching for the next rung on the ladder. When we finally reach the top and peek over the edge, we realize, "Oh, my gosh. I leaned my ladder against the wrong wall... nothing here satisfies me."

Jesus invites us to work with Him and to join ourselves to His yoke.

With this realization comes the knowledge we now have to climb down the ladder and find a different wall to lean it against. I have good news for you. Jesus offers us the perfect, most sure and trustworthy wall. He says:

> *"Come to me, all you who are weary and burdened, and I will give you rest. Take my yoke upon you and learn from me, for I am gentle and humble in heart, and you will find rest for your souls. For my yoke is easy and my burden is light" (Matt. 11:28-30).*

Isn't that beautiful? Jesus promises, "I will give you rest." If you're not familiar with the term, a yoke is a wooden crosspiece fastened over the necks of two animals and attached to the plow or cart they are to pull. When two people are yoked together, it represents a bond between the two parties, as in the yoke of marriage. It is essentially a used as a symbol of a team effort. Jesus invites us to work with Him and to join ourselves to His yoke. He assures us His yoke is easy, and His burden is light. Not only will we learn from Him, and find rest for our weary bodies, but we will find a much deeper rest for our souls.

You might be wondering, *How do I come to Yeshua? How do I accept His yoke?* That answer is easy, by faith. When you're yoked with Him—trusting your life to Him—He will give you what you need for each day. There is an unexplainable blissful rest in this acceptance and it is ultimately what the Sabbath foreshadow is all about.

Maybe the author of Hebrews says it best when referring to the deeper foreshadow meaning of the Sabbath rest:

> *"There remains, then, a Sabbath-rest for the people of God; for anyone who enters God's rest also rests from his own work, just as God did from his" (Heb. 4:9-10).*

Praise God for His rest. I pray you will, if you haven't already, yoke yourself fully to Jesus. He is ready to carry your burdens and give you rest.

The annual Jewish festivals are a strange mix of agrarian and spiritual observances culminating in a week-long celebration. In the Feast foreshadow (my personal favorite), we will find the remaining keys to unveil the mystery of God's plan to establish an eternal family. Pay particular attention to this final foreshadow, because I believe you will receive the deepest and most exciting revelations of God's greater purpose in our lives.

PART VIII

CHAPTER 22

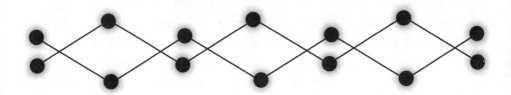

The Feasts, Episode No. 1: Gathering the Crops

It's all about going home.

The Feasts are my favorite foreshadow by far. They are undoubtedly the most exciting of the seven. All of the foreshadows we have explored so far have one common purpose—unveiling the mystery of God's plan to establish an eternal family. The Feasts foreshadow not only has the same purpose, but it also unveils the *completion* of God's plan. It brings closure to God's master plan because the underlying message of the Feasts foreshadow is about *going home*. And as we all know by now, there is no place like home!

On that note, do you know what green jello, gefilte fish, twenty-five-cents per card bingo, and a room full of very chatty Jewish people all have in common?

The answer is, my childhood family gatherings. Trust me, you have never experienced life until you have spent time with my *meshugah* family. Every family has some kind of family-gathering custom, ranging from spontaneous and loose, to annual, and seriously traditional. Every family also has its usual cast of characters who bring more than a little color to those gatherings. For instance, we all have an Aunt Ethel who wears her apron throughout the gathering, making sure everybody has plenty of food. There's little nephew, Bradley, whom you know will throw a tantrum at some point. And Grandpa Bernie, who sits on the couch, slipping in and out of sleep all day. Cousin Lily dominates every conversation with the latest drama going on in her life. Then there's eleven-year-old Johnny, who repeatedly tries to show everyone the same magic trick all day. And who can forget Uncle Louis, who can't wait to tell everyone his latest dirty joke.

Don't we all have similarly colorful characters in our families?

Don't we all have similarly colorful characters in our families?

This seventh and final foreshadow focuses on annual family gatherings and is a strange mix of agrarian and spiritual observances. The Feasts foreshadow begins as a prophetic picture of *gathering the crops* in episode one. It then becomes spiritually fulfilled as *the gathering of souls* in episode two, and it is eternally completed as *a gathering of the family* in episode three. The seven foreshadows make up Biblical Israel, and in this one, we examine the pattern God used to unite His Biblical family. We will see how God commanded Israel to come together for seven annual family gatherings called Feasts or Festivals and learn how this foreshadow will ultimately be realized through eternity. The Seven Feasts of Israel are such overwhelmingly impressive events that some of you may well wonder why you haven't heard this information before. After this chapter, I believe you will understand how God could weave such an intricate story, and then ensure that the story unfolds over the course of history exactly the way He wrote it.

The Book of Ecclesiastes says:

> *"There is a time for everything, and a season for every activity under heaven: a time to be born and a time to die, a time to plant and a time to uproot..." (Ecc. 3:1-2).*

In the Feasts foreshadow, we see a strong spiritual connection between the human life cycle from birth to death and the annual agrarian cycle from planting to uprooting. This is because God built a spiritual message into farming, which is why we find so many Biblical parables are centered around agriculture. There's a hidden spiritual-agricultural message that will be powerfully unveiled in this Feasts foreshadow.

Let's see how God describes each of these seven feasts in episode one. In Leviticus, the Lord instructed Moses, "These are the LORD's appointed feasts, the sacred assemblies you are to proclaim at their appointed times..." (Lev. 23:4). The Hebrew word for "appointed feasts" and "appointed times" is identical, and in its plural form, it is pronounced *moadim*. The word moadim refers to "feasts," to "seasons," and also to "times." The word often conveys the idea that these events are established by God for a highly specific spiritual purpose. Take note that whenever this word is used in the Bible, it is wise to explore its spiritual purpose in more depth because it always has a deeper message to convey. This significant underlying message is exactly what we find when we examine the seven Feasts of the Lord.

These seven Feasts are a seemingly odd mixture of religious and agricultural events, all revolving around the annual agrarian cycle. They are all listed on the chart below:

GOD'S APPOINTED TIMES

This month [nissan] is to be for you the first month, the first month of your year. (Exodus 12:2)

Spring Feasts				
	Passover	Lamb Sacrificed	פסח	Pesach
	Unleavened Bread	No Leaven	חג המצות	Chag HaMatzot
	First Fruits	Early First Fruits	יום הבכורים	Yom Habikkurim
	Weeks	Latter First Fruits	שבועות	Shavuot
Summer Harvest Time				
Fall Feasts				
	Trumpets	Grain Harvest Ends	יום תרועה	Yom Teruah
	Day of Atonement	National Judgment	יום כפור	Yom Kippur
	Booths	Week Celebration	סכות	Sukkot

Figure 2: God's Appointed Times

Notice how Exodus 12:2 in the chart references God's appointed time for the beginning of the year as spring, during the Hebrew month of Nissan, which typically begins in March in our Gregorian calendar. God appointed four seasons to govern our world. In their Biblical order spring comes first, followed by summer, fall, and finally, winter.

Today, modern Israel celebrates the beginning of their year in fall, but they have lost their ancient connection to the Biblical New Year. To appreciate the deeper spiritual meaning of this annual seven-feast cycle, we need to first understand why God appointed spring and not fall to be the beginning of the calendar year for Israel. Starting the cycle in spring makes good sense because spring follows winter and winter is a metaphor for struggle. Vegetation withers and lies dormant, trees lose their leaves, and food becomes scarce. Life comes to a slow, weary crawl during winter. Daily routines become increasingly difficult.

In winter, especially beyond the opulent reach of big cities, we are more likely to consider our daily survival. We ask questions such as, "What if our furnace breaks during a blizzard and we are thirty miles from shelter? Will we survive?" Winter cultivates endurance, faith, and hope, because of our desperate need for spring to arrive, bringing with it warmth and new life. Flowers begin to bloom in spring, animals give birth, and the fresh green shoots of new crops appear. The blooms on the trees remind us that no trial lasts forever, and we feel proud of ourselves for having made it through another grueling season. Life is good again.

What we learn from the pattern of Biblical seasons is a recurring, annual impression of struggle mixed with hope, followed by redemption and abundance. *This* is God's primary intent regarding the annual feast cycle. God appointed spring to be the beginning of the year and He appointed Passover to be the first spring feast.

PESACH (PASSOVER)

Passover (*Pesach* in Hebrew) is a feast that commemorates God delivering the Jewish people from slavery in Egypt. For over 400 years the Israelites were trapped in a punishing winter struggle, conscripted into slavery, and forced to do hard labor. God finally delivered them from slavery when, due to the Pharaoh's stubbornness, God allowed an angel of death to slay every firstborn son in Egypt, including the Pharaoh's. It was the tenth and final plague, sent to ensure Pharaoh's obedience, but also to foreshadow something deeper.

God protected the firstborn sons of the Israelites by instructing every Jewish family to slaughter a perfect and unblemished lamb, using its blood to mark the sides and tops of their doorframes. Doing this ensured the angel of death would pass over the Israelites' homes. To commemorate their salvation, God commanded every Jewish household to sacrifice a lamb each year on Passover. Once the Temple was built, Passover lambs were also sacrificed on the altar between 3:00 p.m. and twilight on the fourteenth of Nissan—the day on which Passover is observed every year (Exod. 12:1–14).

CHAG HAMATZOT
(THE FEAST OF UNLEAVENED BREAD)

On the day following Pesach, the second feast would begin, lasting for seven days. This is the feast called, *Chag HaMatzot*, or the feast of Unleavened Bread. Because the Israelites had to leave Egypt quickly, the bread they took with them was made without yeast. They did not have enough time to allow dough to rise. This fact prompted God to forbid the use of any yeast in Jewish homes, as well as a strict rule to eat nothing made with yeast during the Feast of Unleavened Bread.

Now think about how many products contain yeast. Perhaps it wasn't quite so extreme back in Biblical days but today, many food products contain yeast. This no-yeast rule had to be followed for the entire seven-day period of the feast, and anyone who violated this commandment was to be cut off from the community forever. *Wow!* God made sure Israel understood this was a big deal. We will find out why when we look at the second episode.

YOM HABIKKURIM
(THE FEAST OF FIRST FRUITS)

The third feast is *Yom HaBikkurim* or the Feast of Early First Fruits. This is an early first fruits celebration of barley, with a latter first fruits celebration of wheat, following exactly fifty days later. For the feast of Yom HaBikkurim, God instructed the farmers in Leviticus 23:11 to take a portion of the early first fruits harvest and bring it to the Temple where the High Priest would use these First Fruits to make a wave offering. The obvious idea behind this early wave offering was one of thanksgiving, and also of hope.

If God has been faithful in bringing this early harvest out of the ground to us, He will be faithful to bring the latter harvest out of the ground as well.

God instructed Israel to observe Yom HaBikkurim on the day after the Sabbath that occurs during the Feast of Unleavened Bread. In Israel, the weekly Sabbath is always on a Saturday, so the following day on the Gregorian calendar is always a Sunday. This will be a significant and interesting detail when we reach the second episode.

SHAVUOT (THE FEAST OF WEEKS)

From the Sunday after Yom HaBikkurim, God instructed Israel to count off fifty days, with the fiftieth day marking the fourth Feast—Shavuot, which means "weeks." It is named after the seven weeks taken to count off these days. The seven weeks of counting is called *Sfirat HaOmer*, which means "The Counting of the Omer." This signifies the countdown from the early harvest to an even greater harvest just fifty days later. The fact that God commanded Israel to count off these fifty days is a significant indication that Shavuot is an extremely meaningful event.

Jewish people start each of these fifty days with a specific prayer: *Baruch atah Adonai Elohenu melihk ha-olam asher kidshanu b'mizvohtov v'tzi-vanu al sfirat ha-omer*, translated as, "Blessed art thou, O Lord our God, King of the universe, who has set us apart by Your commandments and has commanded us concerning the counting of the Omer." And then they will say: *Hayom, yom echad l'omer*, which means, "Today is the first day of the Omer." On the second day they'll say the same prayer, followed by, "Today is the second day of the Omer." The countdown will continue every day, all the way through to the fiftieth day. Every day will be counted until Shavuot is reached—the Latter First Fruits celebration marking the beginning of the wheat harvest. Exodus 23:16 refers to this day as "the Feast of the Harvest." Today, the

Jewish people reference Shavuot mostly as the celebration of Moses receiving the Torah because it is believed it took the Israelites fifty days from leaving Egypt to reach Mount Sinai. However, as interesting as this detail is, God's Biblical instructions for Shavuot is connected to celebrating the beginning of harvest season.

Shavuot concludes the four spring feasts. From this point forward through summer, there are no more feasts. You may wonder why. But the reason is quite evident: it is harvest time, and people work during the harvest. There is only a short window of opportunity to bring the harvest in. There is no time to party or celebrate.

YOM TERUAH (THE FEAST OF TRUMPETS)

With the arrival of fall, the fifth feast is celebrated, *Yom Teruah* or the Feast of Trumpets. Today, Yom Teruah is celebrated as *Rosh Hashanna*, the Jewish New Year. Like Shavuot, this feast day has lost much of its original agrarian connection. On the Feast of Trumpets, God commanded the Israelites to blow the shofar all day long. The intention behind this feast is also evident—to mark the end of the grain harvest. One would expect to have a wild harvest celebration in thanks for the bounty God has provided, but as you will see in the ten days leading up to the next feast, this is not the case. And the reason for this gives profound insight into the heart of God if you are paying attention.

YOM KIPPUR (THE DAY OF ATONEMENT)

Ten days after Yom Teruah (celebrated as Rosh Hashanna today), the Feast of *Yom Kippur* is observed. It is the sixth feast in the cycle which is known as The Day of Atonement. During the ten days leading up to Yom Kippur, Jews somberly reflect on their deeds from the previous year and start pleading with God to forgive their shortcomings. This is the feast we covered in detail in the Temple foreshadow. The high priest would take the blood of a goat and enter into the Holy of Holies, where he sprinkled the blood on the Mercy Seat of God, on behalf of the Israelite community. The people would wait anxiously outside the temple walls to see if God would accept their sacrifice. When the high priest emerged unscathed, there was most likely a collective sigh of relief from the crowd.

Isn't it interesting that God inserted this somber moment between the end of the harvest and the subsequent party? Is the Day of Atonement just a random event in the agrarian cycle, or is it an extremely significant foreshadow moment? And could this be the most significant message in this book? The answer to this question will soon be unveiled.

SUKKOT (THE FEAST OF BOOTHS/TABERNACLES)

After the somber self-reflection of Yom Kippur, the seventh and final feast is celebrated: Sukkot—the Feast of Booths or the Feast of Tabernacles. The harvest is over, forgiveness has come, and now it is finally time to truly party. The Feast of Booths is a festive, seven-day harvest celebration. God commanded each Jewish family to build a temporary structure called a *Sukkah*, the singular of Sukkot (booths) in Hebrew. These harvest booths were also to remind the Israelites of their time as sojourners in the wilderness, when God brought them out of Egypt (See Leviticus 23:43). They were to decorate these booths with their harvest bounty: figs, grapes, and whatever other crops had been harvested. The Israelites lived in these temporary structures for seven days, eating and sleeping in the Sukkah, and having friends come over to visit.

At the end of this seven-day festival, winter would set in again, and with it, the questions: "Will we survive the cold? Will we have enough food?" Then the following spring, the agrarian cycle would start all over again and hope would be renewed.

There are two fascinating details regarding these seven feasts. The first is that all four of the spring feasts are spiritually fulfilled in the second episode of God's trilogy and all three of the fall feasts are eternally completed in the third episode. The second detail, even more riveting, is that the fulfillment of these feasts—or at least the first four—all take place on the exact feast day to which they correspond. Not the day before, not the day after, but exactly on the specific moadim or God's appointed feast day.

I suspect the fulfillment of the final three will also correspond to their appointed feast days. But, of course, we will have to wait and see.

CHAPTER 23

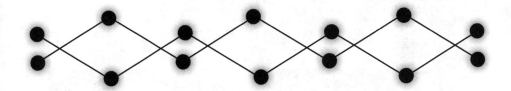

The Feasts, Episode No. 2: Gathering the Souls

N ow we can start answering some of those very intriguing questions. Using the chart below, let's take a look at how the Feasts foreshadow moves from a prophetic picture of gathering the crops to a spiritual fulfillment of gathering the souls.

PESACH (PASSOVER)

EPISODE 2: GATHERING THE SOULS		
Spring Feasts Passover	Lamb Sacrificed	Crucifixion
Unleavened Bread	No Leaven	Burial
First Fruits	Early First Fruits	Resurrection
Weeks	Latter First Fruits	Soul Harvest Begins
Summer Harvest Time		
Fall Feasts Trumpets	Grain Harvest Ends	
Day of Atonement	National Judgment	
Booths	Week Celebration	

Figure 3: Gathering the Souls—Crucifixion

The first of the seven feasts is Passover. The Feast of Passover is spiritually fulfilled by Yeshua's crucifixion. Just as the Feast of Passover details how God delivered the Jewish people from the winter of their physical bondage to the Egyptians, Yeshua's crucifixion details how God delivered us from the winter of our spiritual bondage to sin. Just as the blood of a perfect, unblemished, sacrificial lamb marked the door-frames of Jewish homes to spare the firstborn's life from physical death, so does the blood of the ultimate, unblemished sacrificial Lamb, Yeshua, marked on the door-frames of our hearts, spare our lives from spiritual death.

God delivered us from the winter of our spiritual bondage to sin.

Now, for the first of those riveting details. There is not 100-percent agreement among biblical scholars, but many, including myself, believe Jesus was crucified on Passover during the precise window of time the sacrificial lambs were slaughtered in the Temple. It makes good sense that Jesus would be sacrificed on this special day and to give more credence to this rationale, the scriptures tell us that Jesus took His last breath at 3:00 p.m. in the afternoon—during the precise *window of time* the Passover lambs were slaughtered. This is why 1 Corinthians 5:7 describes Jesus as the Messiah, "...our Passover lamb..." who has been sacrificed. And also why John the Baptist, when he first saw Jesus, said, "...'Look, the Lamb of God, who takes away the sin of the world!'" (John 1:29).

Take note of how God aligned this first feast to correspond perfectly with the actual event it foreshadows. The Messiah's last breath was taken at the precise moment the Passover lambs were being slaughtered. Keep a record of this tally which, so far, puts God one for one concerning the alignment of foreshadow and event to the exact day.

CHAG HAMATZOT (THE FEAST OF UNLEAVENED BREAD)

EPISODE 2: GATHERING THE SOULS			
Spring Feasts	Passover	Lamb Sacrificed	Crucifixion
	Unleavened Bread	No Leaven	Burial
	First Fruits	Early First Fruits	Resurrection
	Weeks	Latter First Fruits	Soul Harvest Begins
Summer Harvest Time			
Fall Feasts	Trumpets	Grain Harvest Ends	
	Day of Atonement	National Judgment	
	Booths	Week Celebration	

Figure 4: Gathering the Souls—Burial

Next is the Feast of Unleavened Bread, and it corresponds to Jesus' burial. It only takes a small amount of yeast to affect an entire batch of dough, and yeast is sometimes (but not always) used as a metaphor for sin in the Bible (3).The Israelites were instructed in the Torah to rid their homes of yeast during the feast of unleavened bread as a way of remembering how they did not have time for their bread to rise when leaving Egypt, however, there is also some obvious symbolism to removing sin. Today, devout Jews spend a feverish week before this feast ensuring there is no trace of any yeast in their homes. Jesus, our Passover Lamb, was perfect, unblemished, and sinless. He took our sins (the yeast) of the world upon Himself when He was buried as all our sins, past, present, and future, were buried with Him. Any trace of sin is forever removed, just like any trace of yeast is removed from homes during the Feast of Unleavened Bread.

Isaiah puts it this way: "He [the Messiah] was assigned a grave with the wicked, and with the rich in his death, though he had done no violence, nor was any deceit in his mouth" (Isa. 53:9). Paul, writing to the Corinthian Church, states the same case in different words: "God made him [the Messiah, Yeshua] who had no sin [no yeast] to be sin [to be yeast] for us, so that in him we might become the righteousness of God" (2 Cor. 5:21). Here is an amazing detail about this feast: Jesus was in His grave during the Feast of Unleavened Bread, taking upon Himself the very sins (yeast) of the world.

This brings God's tally to two for two, regarding the alignment of foreshadow and event to the exact day.

YOM HABIKKURIM (THE FEAST OF FIRST FRUITS)

EPISODE 2: GATHERING THE SOULS			
Spring Feasts	Passover	Lamb Sacrificed	Crucifixion
	Unleavened Bread	No Leaven	Burial
	First Fruits	Early First Fruits	Resurrection
	Weeks	Latter First Fruits	Soul Harvest Begins
Summer Harvest Time			
Fall Feast	Trumpets	Grain Harvest Ends	
	Day of Atonement	National Judgment	
	Booths	Week Celebration	

Figure 5: Gathering the Souls—Resurrection

Third is the Feast of First Fruits, which corresponds to Yeshua's resurrection. This is probably the most important feast for us to know. Most Jews are unaware of this feast, since it is not observed in Judaism today. Most Christians are also unaware of it because the feasts are typically not taught or observed in Christianity. This amazing feast is a beautiful foreshadow of the Resurrection.

According to Leviticus 23:11, the early first fruit wave offering took place the day after the Sabbath during the Feast of Unleavened Bread. That would be Sunday on the Jewish calendar. Now, picture that specific Sunday about 2,000 years ago when the farmers had brought their first fruits to the priest and the priest offered the fruits as a thanksgiving to God. While the priest was declaring how, just as God had been faithful to bring in the early first fruits out of the ground, He will be faithful to bring in the latter out of the ground as well, a very excited Jew comes running down the street shouting, "He is risen! He's risen!"

Can you picture some of the farmers making an immediate connection? This is why the following passage of scripture makes so much sense:

> *"But Christ [Messiah] has indeed been raised from the dead, the firstfruits of those who have fallen asleep. For since death came through a man, the resurrection of the dead comes also through a man. For as in Adam all die, so in Christ [Messiah] all will be made alive. But each in his own turn: Christ [Messiah], the firstfruits; then, when he comes, those who belong to him [the latter first fruits, who are the believers]"* (1 Cor. 15:20-23).

Jesus rose from the dead on the feast of First Fruits which brings God's total tally to three for three.

SHAVUOT (THE FEAST OF WEEKS)

EPISODE 2: GATHERING THE SOULS

Spring Feasts	Passover	Lamb Sacrificed	Crucifixion
	Unleavened Bread	No Leaven	Burial
	First Fruits	Early First Fruits	Resurrection
	Weeks	Latter First Fruits	Soul Harvest Begins
Summer Harvest Time			
Fall Feasts	Trumpets	Grain Harvest Ends	
	Day of Atonement	National Judgment	
	Booths	Week Celebration	

Figure 6: Gathering the Souls—Soul Harvest Begins

Next, from the day of the first fruits, the Israelites counted off the fifty days leading up to Shavuot, marking the beginning of the harvest. Before ascending to Heaven, Jesus told His disciples to wait in Jerusalem for the promised arrival of the Holy Spirit. Being observant Jews, they were no doubt counting off the fifty days from the third feast, Yom HaBikkurim—the Feast of Early First Fruits, to the fourth feast, Shavuot—the Feast of Weeks. Now, as observant Jews, on the morning of the day they were in the upper room, they surely must have prayed the specific prayer they prayed every day between the Feast of First Fruits and the Feast of Weeks—*Baruch atah Adonai Elohenu...* and then they must have numbered the relevant day in their count: *"Today is the fiftieth day of the Omer."* And what do you think happened on day fifty?

The Book of Acts tells us exactly what happened:

> *"When the day of Pentecost [Greek for Shavuot] came, they were all together in one place. Suddenly a sound like the blowing of a violent wind came from heaven and filled the whole house where they were sitting"* (Acts 2:1-2).

We also see the Holy Spirit was sent from our Father in Heaven like a mighty, rushing wind, swooping down in pure love, joy, and power to fill everyone in the upper room. Enabled and empowered by the Spirit of Elohim, they began speaking in foreign languages, unknown to them (reference to Acts 2:3-4).

Thousands of Jews were in Jerusalem for this feast, it being one of three feasts requiring a pilgrimage. Hearing the Spirit-filled believers, some assumed the group in the upper room were drunk. Peter stood to set the record straight, explaining to the crowd that his fellow Jesus-followers were not drunk, as it was only nine o'clock in the morning. He went on to explain that instead, this was what the prophet, Joel, had spoken of concerning the "latter" days:

> *"And it shall come to pass afterward, that I will pour out my Spirit on all flesh; your sons and your daughters shall prophesy, your old men shall dream dreams, and your young men shall see visions. Even on the male and female servants in those days I will pour out my Spirit" (Joel 2:28-29).*

When he was finished preaching, Peter gave the first invitation and 3,000 of these Jewish pilgrims put their faith in Yeshua (Acts 2:41).

Following their acceptance of Jesus as Messiah, they were immediately immersed (baptized) in the mikvot (ritual cleansing pools) located outside the entrance of the temple by the Southern Steps. This ritual, already familiar to observant Jews, demonstrated publicly they were now followers of Rabbi Yeshua. Again, God had perfectly orchestrated the alignment between the (Shavuot) foreshadow and the actual event (soul harvest) it predicted. On the exact day the gathering of the latter crops was being celebrated, the gathering of the souls began. Now we know why God commanded Israel to count off the fifty days to Shavuot. It foreshadowed the body of Messiah which is commonly called the Church today.

This brings God's tally to four for four regarding the spring feasts.

NO FEASTS DURING HARVEST TIME

Here is possibly the most interesting, and certainly the most critical part of this feast, from this point forward, all the way through summer, there are no feasts as it is harvest time. This means the current event displayed on our spiritual calendar is also harvest time. In the realm of Spirit, there will be no more feasts until our spiritual summer is over. Why? Because everyone must work during harvest time. This is why Jesus said:

> "...The harvest is plentiful but the workers are few. Ask the Lord of the harvest, therefore, to send out workers into his harvest field" (Matthew 9:37-38).

We clearly see we are in the spiritual harvest season, not celebration, or relaxing or partying. Not only are we instructed to gather souls to increase our Heavenly family (See Matthew 28:19-20), we are also instructed to pray for more harvest laborers to work alongside us.

And now it's time for the fall feasts, which, from what I can discern in scripture, hold some exciting spiritual foreshadows.

CHAPTER 24

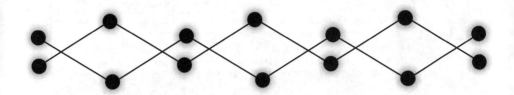

The Feasts, Episode No. 3: Gathering the Family

Finally, we have come to the fall feasts, which is where the Feasts foreshadow goes from being spiritually fulfilled as the gathering of souls in episode two, to being eternally completed as a gathering of the family, in episode three. As I alluded to in the previous section, these fulfillments will not happen until we reach the third and final episode of the story. Because this family gathering takes place in the future, there is no way of being sure these final three feast events will occur on the exact dates of the Earthly feasts to which they correspond. My best guess is that they will. Here's why:

YOM TERUAH (THE FEAST OF TRUMPETS)

EPISODE 2: GATHERING THE SOULS

Spring Feasts	Passover	Lamb Sacrificed	Crucifixion
	Unleavened Bread	No Leaven	Burial
	First Fruits	Early First Fruits	Resurrection
	Weeks	Latter First Fruits	Soul Harvest Begins
Summer Harvest Time			
Fall Feast	Trumpets	Grain Harvest Ends	Soul Harvest Begins
	Day of Atonement	National Judgment	Global Judgment
	Booths	Week Celebration	Eternal Celebration

Figure 7: Gathering the Family: Soul Harvest Ends

The fifth feast is Yom Teruah, the Feast of Trumpets. This feast was marked by blowing the shofar for a full day; it marks the end of the grain harvest. What then, will mark the end of the soul harvest? Take a look at Paul's first epistle to the Corinthian Church:

> *"Listen, I tell you a mystery: We will not all sleep, but we will all be changed— in a flash, in the twinkling of an eye, at the last trumpet. For the trumpet will sound, the dead will be raised imperishable, and we will be changed. For the perishable must clothe itself with the imperishable, and the mortal with immortality. When the perishable has been clothed with the imperishable, and the mortal with immortality, then the saying that is written will come true: 'Death has been swallowed up in victory'" (1 Cor. 15:51-54).*

For even more clarification, 1 Thessalonians 4:16-17 says:

> *"For the Lord himself will come down from heaven, with a loud command, with the voice of the archangel and with the trumpet call of God, and the dead in Christ will rise first. After that, we who are still alive*

and are left will be caught up together with them in the clouds to meet the Lord in the air. And so we will be with the Lord forever."

Yes, the end of the final harvest of souls will be announced with the blowing of trumpets. The only thing we aren't told is when this spiritual soul harvest will occur. A passage from Revelation gives us an impression of how this final harvest will be reaped:

"Then another angel came out of the temple and called in a loud voice to him who was sitting on the cloud, 'Take your sickle and reap, because the time to reap has come, for the harvest of the earth is ripe.' So he who was seated on the cloud swung his sickle over the earth, and the earth was harvested" (Rev. 14:15-16).

I think we can agree this passage is certainly not describing a grain harvest. Will the spiritual harvest of souls arrive on the Feast of Trumpets? We will have to wait and see, but, if it does, this will bring God's tally to five for five.

YOM KIPPUR (THE DAY OF ATONEMENT)

EPISODE 2: GATHERING THE SOULS

Spring Feasts	Passover	Lamb Sacrificed	Crucifixion
	Unleavened Bread	No Leaven	Burial
	First Fruits	Early First Fruits	Resurrection
	Weeks	Latter First Fruits	Soul Harvest Begins
Fall Feast			
Fall Feast	Trumpets	Grain Harvest Ends	Soul Harvest Begins
	Day of Atonement	National Judgment	Global Judgment
	Booths	Week Celebration	Eternal Celebration

Figure 8: Gathering the Family—Global Judgment

And again, as with the crop harvest in the annual Yom Teru-ah feast, the soul harvest is not immediately followed by a joyous celebration. The soul harvest celebration is also delayed, but this time by a time of The Great Judgment. Revelation gives us more detail with regard to how this final judgment take place:

> *"And I saw the dead, great and small, standing before the throne, and books were opened [plural—more than one book]. Another book was opened [singular, a different book], which is the book of life [there is a dif-ferentiation between these two books]. The dead were judged according to what they had done as recorded in the books [their deeds are recorded in the books]. The sea gave up the dead that were in it, and death and Ha-des gave up the dead that were in them, and each per-son was judged according to what he had done. Then death and Hades were thrown into the lake of fire. The lake of fire is the second death" (Rev. 20:12-14).*

The next verse does not sound pleasant: "If anyone's name was *not found* written in The Book of Life, he was thrown into the lake of fire" (Rev. 20:15). Again, this matches the agrarian parallels found in the life of Yeshua. John the Baptist said this of Him:

> *"His winnowing fork is in his hand, and he will clear his threshing floor, gathering his wheat into the barn and burning up the chaff with unquenchable fire" (Matt. 3:12).*

This gives us a clear understanding of what will happen at the end of this age, when God finally brings this chapter of Earth's history to an end just moments before its new beginning in New Jerusalem. Every person who has ever walked the Earth will go up before the judgment seat—the Great White Throne of God. This will truly be the mother of all Yom Kippurs. It will be a judgment of historical proportions. We will ultimately be judged by one of these two record books that scripture tells us God keeps.

The first is titled, The Book of Deeds, and it contains everything you and I have ever done in our lives, both good and bad. The second book is titled, The Book of Life. In Revelation 21:27, the second book is called The Lamb's Book of Life, so I suppose it contains all the deeds Jesus has done for us. I believe this means that we will either be judged by our works or by Jesus' works—by the Book of Deeds or the Book of Life, and the choice is one hundred percent ours to make. Trust me, you want to be judged by Jesus' perfect deeds, not your imperfect ones.

Now, if the Great White Throne Judgment takes place on Yom Kippur, this will bring God's tally to six for six.

Knowing we will be judged makes it easier to understand why God inserted this somber moment between the end of the harvest and the harvest party. The Day of Atonement was not just a random event in the agrarian cycle, it was

Every person who has ever walked the Earth will go up before the judgment seat.

an extremely significant foreshadow of the Great White Throne Judgment that will take place in episode three. Those who choose to accept and live by Yeshua's atoning sacrifice will attend the eternal party of the harvest celebration, paralleling the final agrarian feast of Sukkot. This celebration will take place not in man-made booths, lasting only seven days, but rather it will be held in style in the equivalent of the New Jerusalem Hilton Hotel, and will last forever.

SUKKOT (THE FEAST OF BOOTHS/TABBERNACLES)

EPISODE 2: GATHERING THE SOULS			
Spring Feasts	Passover	Lamb Sacrificed	Crucifixion
	Unleavened Bread	No Leaven	Burial
	First Fruits	Early First Fruits	Resurrection
	Weeks	Latter First Fruits	Soul Harvest Begins
Summer Harvest Time			
Fall Feast	Trumpets	Grain Harvest Ends	Soul Harvest Begins
	Day of Atonement	National Judgment	Global Judgment
	Booths	Week Celebration	Eternal Celebration

Figure 9: Gathering the Family—Eternal Celebration

In light of this, Jesus made apparent what His followers could expect when He returned for them:

> *"In my Father's house are many rooms; if it were not so, I would have told you. I am going there to prepare a place for you. And if I go and prepare a place for you, I will come back and take you to be with me that you also may be where I am" (John 14:2-3).*

Isn't that powerful? Not only are the "rooms" a foreshadow of the Bridal chamber as discussed in Chapter Four's Covenant Foreshadow, but every believer will have their own eternal Sukkah. And these Sukkot will not be decorated with grapes, figs or wheat. We will be the latter harvest fruit decorating the halls of Heaven. Every tribe, every tongue, and every nation will be present. The family of God will finally have arrived home to live with Him forever—*the foreshadow of Feasts is all about going home.* God has established His eternal family.

Finally, if this eternal celebration coincides with the timing of Sukkot, the Feast of Booths—and I believe it will—this will bring God's final tally to seven for seven.

Would you agree the perfectly orchestrated timing of God's first four appointed feasts is amazing? My Biblically educated guess is, the last three spiritual feasts will also coincide with the last three Earthly festival foreshadows. Who else, but God could do this? Who could arrange the perfect timing of such intricately detailed happenings over the entire course of history?

WE'RE NOT YET HOME

But before we close this captivating chapter, let us consider one last verse: "The harvest is past, the summer has ended, and we are not saved" (Jer. 8:20). The context for this verse most likely relates to the first season through which the Jewish people had lived in exile in Babylon. They would spend another sixty-nine years there, and would spend many more agrarian yearly cycles in Babylon. In this rather poignant verse, Jeremiah is pointing out that one season has gone by and God's people have not yet been rescued as they are still in Babylon and not yet home. I believe this verse offers a relevant foreshadow for us today as we are not yet home either.

One thing I know for certain though is that the wedding invitations have already been sent out, and all we have to do is R.S.V.P. After all, you really don't want to be the one saying, "The harvest is past, the summer has ended, and I am still not saved!" You're invited. I'm invited. We're all invited to this eternal family gathering.

Following Jesus means one has a very inclusive faith.

I often hear people say Christianity is a very exclusive faith. That is not the case. Following Jesus means one has a very inclusive faith. It is, in fact, so easy to be saved. All one must do is accept the Father's invitation, and by faith, not by your works, you will be saved. Simple faith in Yeshua and the work He has done for you through the cross will have you welcomed with open arms to the family gathering. You will know you are saved when you recognize family members here on Earth. I promise you, your deeds will get you nowhere. It is by grace alone, that all of us have been saved, and it is through our faith we are saved, not by our works. This prevents us from boasting about what we can do, and it allows us to focus on what Jesus has already done for us.

So, what we do with all this information? How do we apply these seven foreshadows to our daily lives, so we can be better prepared for the real-life events to which they point us? And how do we apply our newfound knowledge of the seven feasts of the Lord? Will you please allow your knowledge of the first four to dictate how you prepare for the next three? In the final chapter we explore answers to these questions. We also consider our own personal stories, reflecting on how our individual journeys of faith have become such important pieces of the bigger spiritual puzzle of God's story.

Hopefully, you will enjoy placing the final piece of this foreshadow mystery into the appropriate slot in your heart and mind. I certainly have enjoyed sharing my understanding of God's trilogy about His romantic, all-encompassing story. I think, perhaps, I have enjoyed it so much because I know, as we all do, that everyone loves a great story. Enjoy the last leg of the journey.

PART
IX

PART

XI

CHAPTER 25

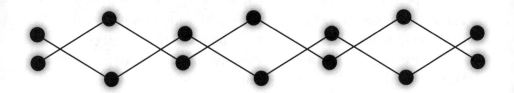

Coming Out of the Shadows

*"Every person of faith has an epic
God-story to tell."*
—Gene Binder)

After exploring the seven major foreshadows displayed through Biblical Israel, something profound takes place. When we *ponder* and then *apply* the lessons we have learned, the spiritual realities of these foreshadows begin to manifest in our own lives. As such, you can consider these seven foreshadows as tools to understand the exquisite truth of God's master plan through the ages.

In this light, this final chapter is about how our story—our individual journey of faith—makes a vital contribution to the telling of God's story. That is why I believe with all my heart the journey is just as important as the destination.

Don't you love great love stories—especially the ones in which the hero comes to save the day? Think about which heroic love story is your personal favorite. Some of us enjoy these stories while curling up on the couch with a good book, while others prefer watching them on film in theaters. Or even live performances on stage.

We love hero love stories that inspire us, scare us, and make us laugh or make us cry. We savor stories where people overcome incredible challenges, in movies like *The Revenant* or in books like *The Grapes of Wrath*. We revel in sagas like *Star Wars* and *The Hunger Games*, where good triumphs over evil. We appreciate stories where the hero sacrifices his life to save others, such as in *The Titanic* or *Braveheart*.

But why is it that we are drawn to these kind of stories? Especially when we know the plotline and likely the ending outcome? While the characters and situations may change from movie to movie, the typical plot usually begins by connecting us emotionally to the main characters. Then the music turns dark and the diabolical antagonist appears, causing anxiety. His nefarious shenanigans give rise to the appearance of the superhero, whose role it is to defeat the villain and rescue the heroine. Having conquered all obstacles and achieved his goal, the story is finally resolved. We then witness the famous tear-jerking scene wherein the hero and the heroine ride off into the sunset to live happily ever after.

Is the "happily ever after scene" really the end of the story? Aren't we left to imagine a new beginning where life will be perfect for the hero and heroine forevermore? I believe we are so accustomed to the pattern behind these hero love stories because they are microcosms of the larger hero love story. They reflect the "Big Story" written by God. It is essentially the meta-narrative, the story about the story, and in a sense, superimposed upon, all the other micro-stories.

As we know, God wrote a beautiful love story before the beginning of time and every one of us is used as a feature character in this story as we are the Messiah's Bride. The satanic antagonist made an early appearance in the Garden of Eden, causing untold chaos. Our Superhero—God—defeated this villain on the cross, and will one day enforce His complete victory over our enemy. On the day we are finally rescued by our Beloved, we will ride off into the sunset, or perhaps meet Him in the clouds to live happily ever after with Him. So that's the end, right?

Wrong. We must remember this classic ride into the sunset is always symbolic of a new beginning and the start of an eternally perfect life. Whether we believe in God or not, authors, scriptwriters, songwriters, and poets keep producing smaller narratives of God's meta-narrative. Time and time again, they keep reflecting this one pattern expressing the essence of their Maker because we are all made in the image of God. His story is engrained in us whether we recognize it or not.

> God wrote a beautiful love story before the beginning of time.

ETERNITY IS WITHIN US

Genesis tells us that God's divine imprint is embedded into our being: "So God created man in his own image, in the image of God he created him; male and female he created them" (Gen. 1:27). This is what separates us from all other species on our planet. This is why throughout our history, at any given location around the world, we find evidence of humans worshiping something—either an inanimate object, a human artifact, or a perceived entity they deem divine. Some cultures have worshiped the sun, a pile of rocks, or prefer to worship their ancestors. Many cultures, both ancient and modern, have also devoutly dedicated themselves to the worship of fame and money.

The truth is, we are all worshipping something and it is common to hear people say, "I believe in this" or "I believe in that." Some people even choose to say, "I don't believe in anything," and this is another fact that sets us apart from other species on this planet—we are given choice. We can believe in something or we can choose to believe in nothing.

This choice is what causes us to think and live differently to all the other species. My dog, Buddy, never comes up to me and says, "What's the meaning of life?" or "I feel dissatisfied with my life." All Buddy really cares about is when he eats and where he sleeps. Only humans probe into deeper questions like, "Why am I here? What is my purpose?" or "What should I be doing with my life?" We ask these questions because we are made in God's image.

> **Time is what keeps us from seeing the whole story from beginning to end.**

A verse from Ecclesiastes informs us that God has added eternity into our being: "...He (God) has also set eternity in the hearts of men; yet they cannot fathom what God has done from beginning to end" (Ecc. 3:11). The question to ask of this verse is, "We can't fathom what God has done from the beginning to the end of *what*?" And the answer is, "From the beginning to the end of *God's story*."

I really enjoy the wordplay between "His Story" and "history." God created time, which gives rise to history, building the "when" factor into the timing of His story. We have a frame of reference when asking, "When did it happen?" In the first, second, or third episode of *His* story? As humans, we are all stuck in time and have no influence over it. Because we are caught up in the entropic web of space, matter, and time, you and I have only a short role in this crazy story. Because we currently exist within the constraints of time, our life on Earth is really short compared to the unknown, timeless eons involved in God's story. Ironically, time is what keeps us from seeing the whole story from beginning to end, but the Author of the big story lives outside of time. God is not confined to time meaning He can see every detail of the story at any point in the timeline He chooses.

Even though we cannot see the whole story from beginning to end, God made us in His image and set eternity in our hearts. We therefore have embedded in us the spiritual knowledge of a divine Creator and as a result, we have a sense that our core being will exist beyond this life. These immutable facts give rise to us writing our own stories and asking deep, philosophical questions. These stories and questions all flow from the meta-narrative embedded in our being. Intuitively, we know there is more to life than the physical world we live in.

This is fascinating when you think about it because God has given us the Bible, which is ultimately a sneak preview of the whole story. The Bible can, in a sense, be compared to a spiritual *Reader's Digest* version of the *Big Story*.

To help us discover the deeper meaning and purpose of life, God tapped a very special group of people—the nation of Israel—to play the role of His Biblical family in the Big Story. In this story, the Jewish people provide an accurate, prophetic roadmap showing us where God's story is headed. When we recognize the potential of these seven major foreshadows, we unveil the mystery of God's plan to establish an eternal family. There are many dimensions to God's story, but building a family of faith to live with Him forever is His primary goal.

THE LIFE CYCLE JOURNEY

By examining the seven foreshadows that make up Biblical

Israel, we see the elegant brilliance of God's plan fulfilled in three nail-biting episodes.

This pattern follows the three-stage progressive nature of God described in Revelation: "the God who was [in episode one], the God who is [in episode two], and the God who is to come [in episode three]" (paraphrase of Rev. 4:8).

Collectively, these seven foreshadows describe God's unconditional and everlasting relationship with Israel. He will fulfill all the promises He made to Abraham and his descendants. They will have a family as numerous as the stars of the sky and a family home called the Promised Land.

Individually, each of these foreshadows tells the Gospel story. The chart below shows the seven foreshadows as they unfold over each of the three episodes, past, present, and future.

CONNECTING THE DOTS
Seven Bible Mysteries You May Have Missed That Will Change Your Life

THE COVENANT [marriage] Till death do us part		
The Engagement	The Reconciliation	The Wedding
THE NATION OF ISRAEL [family] The family is where the story begins and love never ends		
One Nation Under God	One New Man Under God	One Multitude Under God
THE PROMISED LAND [family home] The best journeys always lead back home		
God's Kingdom in Israel	God's Kingdom in Us	God's Kingdom in Eternity
THE TORAH [family rules] Perfect love rules without rules		
Rules for Imperfect Hearts	Rules for New Hearts	No Rules for Perfect Hearts
THE TEMPLE [family access to dad] The best gift a father can give his children is his time		
Distant Access	Confident Access	Full Access
THE SABBATH [weekly family time] True rest is not found in being idle, but in being purposeful		
Ceasing One Day From our Work	Ceasing Everyday From Our Work	Ceasing Forever From Our Work
THE FEASTS [annual family gatherings] It's all about going home		
Gathering the Crops	Gathering the Souls	Gathering the Family

Figure 10: Connecting The Dots Chart

The important concept to grasp about these seven foreshadows are the pictures they create. That is, the *individual* picture, and the *collective* picture of the redemptive and transformative gospel theme flowing through every episode of God's story. What can we do to come out of the shadows? It is only when we understand how we fit into the foreshadowed context of this current episode that we are able to see how our individual faith journey plays an important role in God's story. As journalist Alex Tizon once said, "…all people have within them an epic story." I believe this is true because God has personally written each of our "epic" stories.

Our individual journeys of faith tell beautiful stories of redemption and transformation. And when we understand our own transformation, we point others to the path of redemption.

Our individual journeys of faith tell beautiful stories of redemption and transformation.

I want to help you come out of the shadows by describing two life-defining narratives common to everyone's journey of faith. Before I do this, let me first pose some questions:

- If God's ultimate plan is to establish an eternal family, why must we first experience this journey called life?

- If God's ultimate plan is for us to be with Him in eternity, why do we first have to live on Earth in a physical body?

- Why can't we skip episodes one and two and just go straight to eternity?

I believe the answer to these questions is that there are certain crucial criteria we must first experience in this *finite life* to ensure we are fit for *eternal life*. By looking at these two life-defining narratives you will gain a better understanding of this answer.

The first life-defining narrative is what I call the "life cycle journey," which revolves around what our bodies experience between birth and death. Ecclesiastes tells us, "There is a time for everything, and a season for every activity under heaven: a time to be born and a time to die..." (Ecc. 3:1–2).

As we all know, when we are outside of the womb, we all begin our lives with inspiration. We breathe in and then we all end our lives with expiration as we breathe out. I find this little detail that connects our breathing to life and death rather interesting. Life is an exciting and challenging adventure and at birth we are inspired to begin this adventure. At death, with our final breath, the adventure expires. We reach our expiration date. The detail I find really intriguing is that in between our birth and death we all have to continually breathe in and breathe out. *We must consistently inspire and expire just to remain alive.*

So philosophically speaking, our lives are a mixture of victory and defeat, satisfaction and disappointment, accomplishment and failure, acquisition and loss, beauty and tragedy. And the human life cycle is just one aspect of how we perceive this dichotomy in action. God could have created us as fully mature adults but He didn't. The physiological and emotional adjustments required to transition through the various stages of life are extremely exciting at times, but also strenuously challenging at other times.

As a pastor of a congregation with many families, I have had the privilege of seeing babies grow into kids and then into teens. I have been in this ministry for long enough to see some of them become adults. Their growth spurts are often rapid and I sometimes look at them and ask, "Does that hurt?"

And in reality, yes, it literally does hurt, both physically and emotionally. It hurts when we mature through the cycle of life.

This first life-defining narrative explains why we cannot just go straight into eternity. It hurts to have our teeth push through tender gums. It hurts when we suffer from allergies, catch the flu, break a bone, or try to beat cancer. It hurts when we struggle with anxiety or fear, when we grow older and lose our vitality, experience a stroke or a heart-attack, and it hurts to cope with dementia as we try to hold on to the one thing so dear to us—the memories of our own story.

In God's infinite wisdom He didn't choose to create us as fully mature adults. Instead, we are born into God's story as infants, and we are forced to journey through these various stages of life, in a fallen world, as we continually inspire and expire through our journey. Our physical journey teaches us crucial lessons that prepare us for eternity. This is perhaps what 2 Corinthians is pointing to by referencing the challenges of growing old:

> *"Therefore we do not lose heart. Though outwardly we are wasting away, yet inwardly we are being renewed day by day. For our light and momentary troubles are achieving for us an eternal glory that far outweighs them all. So we fix our eyes not on what is seen, but on what is unseen. For what is seen is temporary, but what is unseen is eternal" (2 Cor. 4:16-18).*

Our bodies are merely a temporary housing for our spirits. We can't take our physical bodies with us into eternity. As our bodies move closer to their expiration date through physically wasting away, our souls become more inspired each day as we are inwardly being renewed. This is because part of growing old is letting go of this physical world so we can take hold of the spiritual world to come.

As we reach the ripe end of maturity, we recognize how, one by one, our physical faculties deteriorate. Our health is diminished, our minds deteriorate, and at some point we realize life just has to be about something else—something much more than the physical. In this sense, the life cycle narrative prepares us for eternity.

THE LIFE EXPERIENCE JOURNEY

This brings us to the second life-defining narrative. I call this the "life experience journey," which is what our souls experience between birth and death. Life clearly carries great grief and many trials of which the apostle Peter speaks to when he says:

> *"These have come so that your faith—of greater worth than gold, which perishes even though refined by fire—may be proved genuine and may result in praise, glory and honor when Jesus Christ [Messiah Yeshua] is revealed" (1 Peter 1:7).*

Peter is referencing the goldsmith's refining process which, by subjecting gold to intense heat, naturally removes impurities. Peter compares the natural process to the spiritual process God uses to refine our faith. Both faith and gold have to go through the intense heat of the refiner's fire to be purified. This entire faith-refining process is in preparation for when Messiah comes to establish His eternal kingdom in the third and final episode of God's story.

Now, what I love most about this passage is that Peter wrote it. If anyone needed to be refined more in his lifetime, it is this formerly arrogant, condescending, know-it-all, named Peter. Do you know a person of faith like this? If you don't, take a good look in the mirror because it might be you. This is a person who has a super-spiritual, holier-than-thou attitude. He is someone who has all the answers for every question. He is someone who sees everything as black and white, right or wrong, with no gray areas in life at all. He will give you his opinion about it, whether you ask for it or not. The lives of these characters are typically a mess, and they are often some of the biggest hypocrites around. This was the stereotype of the pre-crucifixion Peter.

When Jesus talked about His suffering and imminent death in Matthew's gospel, Peter pulled Jesus aside and basically said to Him, "What the heck are You talking about? That's not how it goes down!" (paraphrase of Matt. 16:22). Bear in mind, Peter was talking to God. Can you believe the *chutzpah* this guy had?

Jesus, being a no-nonsense kind of guy Himself, immediately shot back at Peter: "Get behind me, Satan! You are a stumbling block to me; you do not have in mind the things of God, but the things of men" (Matt. 16:23). This response must have sharply resonated with Peter.

Ten chapters later, a few hours before Jesus was arrested, He told His disciples they would all run away when He was arrested, but super-spiritual Peter quickly proclaimed: "Even if all fall away on account of you, I never will" (Matt. 26:33).

Jesus answered him, saying, "Let me tell you what's really going down here, Peter; this night—this very night—before the rooster crows you will disown Me. Not just once, Peter, but three times. You'll have three opportunities to get this right, but you will fail every time" (paraphrase of Matt. 26:34).

Peter, of course, in his brash and impetuous manner, insisted yet again he knew himself better than Jesus did, saying, "Even if I have to die with you, I will never disown you..." (Matt. 26:35).

Later that night, of course, Peter denied Jesus three times. Luke describes the moment Peter denied Jesus for the third time:

> *"Peter replied, 'Man, I don't know what you're talking about!' Just as he was speaking, the rooster crowed. The Lord turned and looked straight at Peter. Then Peter remembered the word the Lord had spoken to him: 'Before the rooster crows today, you will disown me three times.' And he went outside and wept bitterly"* (Luke 22:60-62).

At the exact moment of his denial, Jesus made eye contact with Peter. Can you imagine how Peter must have felt? Immediately, Peter left the courtyard, weeping bitterly. All the gospel writers tell this story, but only Doctor Luke tells us that Peter wept bitterly. This is a crucial detail—it is one of those life-defining, game-changing moments for Peter. He is humiliated and his pride is finally broken. He realizes he is no super-spiritual giant. He appears to be what he seems to hate the most—a spiritual fraud.

The moment Jesus caught Peter's eye, mid-denial, Peter entered into the intense heat of the refiner's fire so the impurities of his faith could be removed.

Later the same day, Jesus was crucified. After He had risen from the dead three days later, Jesus appeared to His disciples several times over the next forty days, before ascending back to Heaven. Even though Peter had met with Jesus during that time, he was probably wondering, *Am I not fit to be a follower of Jesus? My time has expired.*

And so, in the final chapter of John's gospel, it looks like Peter has gone back to fishing for fish instead of for men. Isn't it interesting how typical this is for all of us? We so quickly want to fall back into old lifestyles in the face of our failures and disappointments. It happens all too often

Peter went back to fishing and some of the other disciples joined him, but after staying out on the lake all night, they had not caught a single fish. A familiar, yet unknown voice from the shoreline, having established they had not caught any fish, called out to them, saying, "Throw your net on the right side of the boat and you will find some" (John 21:6). Acting on the stranger's advice, they were unable to haul the net in because of the large number of fish it held. This interaction was similar to what had happened when Peter and John first met Jesus, that they realized it was Jesus calling to them from the shoreline and rushed back to the shore to meet Him.

This reunion, while generating great excitement, was no doubt awkward for Peter. He and Jesus hadn't yet had a chance to discuss how Peter's denial was so contrary to his initial bravado. Maybe Peter was even thinking, *This must be the moment He's going to kick me off the team.*

But after sharing a meal of fish and bread, Jesus created an opportunity. He broke the ice and said to Peter, "Hey, Peter, do you really love Me more than the other disciples?" (paraphrase of John 21:15).

Jesus was obviously referring back to the time when Peter foolishly, naively exclaimed, "Even if everyone abandons You, I'll never abandon You. I'll go to my death for You!"

In a sense, Jesus was asking Peter, "Are you still clueless or have you learned something?" Because Peter denied Jesus three times, Jesus asked him this same question three times, and each time Peter affirmed his love for Jesus. What you can't tell from the English biblical translation is the two different Greek words used for the word, "love" in this dialogue.

English only has one word for love, but the Greek language has three:

Agape is an unconditional type of love, and is used to express the kind of love God has for people and the love we should have for God. It is the kind of love that enables people to willingly die for the subject of their love. It is the kind of love Jesus expressed for us by dying on the cross.

Phileo is an expression of good friendship, but probably not the best word to describe a friend who would willingly take a bullet for you.

Eros is an erotic or sexual kind of love and is not applicable in this case, but is worth bearing in mind when considering the genesis of meaning behind "love."

The conversation between Jesus and Peter bounces back and forth between the use of agape and phileo. Below, I have inserted these two words as they appear in their conversation for you to see which one is being used. When Jesus asked the question the first time, He said, "Peter, do you *agape* me? Do you love me like you professed earlier, so much you would willingly go to your death for Me?" (paraphrase of John 21:15).

To which Peter replied, "I *phileo* love you. I love you like a good friend" (paraphrase of John 21:15).

Jesus responded by saying, "...Feed my lambs" (John 21:15). Then Jesus asked a second time, "Peter, do you *agape* Me? Will you die for Me? Do you love me so much, so unconditionally, that you will die for Me?" (paraphrase of John 21:16).

Again, Peter said, "I love you, Lord. I *phileo* love You. I love You as a close friend" (paraphrase of John 21:16).

This time Jesus responded by saying, "...Take care of my sheep" (John 21:16).

The third time Jesus asked this question of Peter, He modified it saying, "Peter do you love Me like a friend? Do you *phileo* love me?" (paraphrase of John 21:17).

Understandably, Peter became a little defensive: "You know this is how I love You, Lord. You knew it when You asked the question the first time... this is all I have. I wish I had more, but this is all I have to give You" (paraphrase of John 21:17).

Peter's telling reply reveals he is no longer a super-spiritual, arrogant, clueless, follower of Jesus. He had become more authentic, more transparent, and more down to Earth. He had become more relatable, and my guess is, he no longer had an answer for everything. What I love about this conversation is, each time Peter says, "I only *phileo* love You, Jesus," Jesus responds positively, saying to Peter:

"Awesome. I can use a broken, self-aware guy like you. Feed my sheep."

From this day forward, Peter was a changed man who did spectacular things for the kingdom of God. His faith ultimately proved to be a genuine faith that was fit for eternity.

This is Peter's story, but what is your story?

Psalm 139, referencing God's book, says, "...All the days ordained for me were written in your book before one of them came to be" (Psa. 139:16). God wrote a moving, three-part story but His story is incomplete without your story. Like Peter's, your story is the redemptive and transformative work God is doing on your journey of faith to make you fit for eternity.

FIT FOR ETERNITY

In conclusion, I will present one final story from the Bible to illustrate how important our stories are in God's great trilogy. John's gospel includes the story of an adult man who had been blind since birth. In Jewish thinking – the rabbinic teaching in Jesus' day—if you had an affliction of this nature, it was a reflection of one's connection to sin. So Jesus' disciples asked Him, "Rabbi, who sinned? Was it this man or his parents, that he was born blind?" (John 9:2). Their question poses another, "How could he have sinned in the womb?"

Jesus replied: "Neither this man nor his parents sinned... but this happened so that the work of God might be displayed in his life" (John 9:3).

Remember the Psalm that puts into perspective God's master plan and how we fit into His greater story? "All the days ordained for you and I were written in God's book, His story, before even one of those days ever came to be" (paraphrase of Psa. 139:16).

Now, it happened to be the Sabbath when Jesus healed this man who had been blind since his birth. We know from the Sabbath foreshadow that healing on the Sabbath was unacceptable in rabbinic teaching. The Pharisees started harassing the man who had received his sight. After hearing his story, they then badgered his parents, asking them how their son had been healed. His parents were terrified to answer, knowing what the Pharisees thought of Jesus, so they said their son was of age, and he could speak for himself.

The Pharisees then approached the man a second time, saying,

"...Give glory to God... We know this man is a sinner." (John 9:24).

Having consistently pressed this guy into telling them what they wanted to hear, he had finally had enough of their accusatory insinuations and said, "...Whether he is a sinner or not, I don't know. One thing I do know. I was blind but now I see!" (John 9:25). It seems as if he is saying to the Pharisees, "Look, I'm not going to allow you to put me into a theological compartment of your making. There's only one thing I know and that is that I used to be blind, but now I can see. That's my story!"

What is your story?

As believers, our stories are individual and wonderfully unique, but they all display the redemptive and transformative work of God on our journey to faith. He is making us fit for eternity. But without your story, God's story is incomplete. You are a living, breathing testimony, and the best way to tell your story is just the way this man told his: "I used to be blind, but now I see. I don't really know all the technical details involved. It could have something to do with predestination, or maybe even free will. These are interesting topics to discuss but the simple truth is that I used to be a certain way, but now I'm a very different person and I only have God to thank for my transformation."

Bless the Lord, O My Soul.

Epilogue: A Closing Prayer

As we conclude our journey through these foreshadows, my hope is you have gained something that will bring you closer to Yeshua. That is my deepest desire. If you don't know Him, all I can say is that it is time to come home. What exactly does that mean? Well, it means a lot of different things for a lot of different people, but maybe for the first time, you are hearing there is a different home from the home you currently live in. Maybe you thought, like I did thirty-five years ago, that you live this life, you die, and that is it. However, I pray you are persuaded that there is something more now and that you want to ensure you will live in your eternal home—the place Yeshua wants to prepare for you. It begins by you saying, "Yes, I want to live by faith. Thank you, Yeshua, for paying the price for my sins with your own life. I love You because You first loved me. I'm in!"

Or maybe you're not at peace or you're not settled and there are things going on in your life preventing you from being in that place. Maybe it is your home life, your work life, or your relationships that are not allowing you to feel like you are at home.

That said, I want to provide an opportunity for you. Whatever home means for you today, whatever the Holy Spirit is saying to you about home, I want you to come home.

Here is my prayer for you:

> "Father, I pray that You bless these readers who see You as the Father sitting by the window waiting for His son or daughter to come home. No one is more excited about us coming home than You. As such, we want to come home as our hearts long to be with yours. Yeshua said in Matthew 11:28, 'Come to me all who are weary

and burdened and I will give you rest for your souls.'
This is about soul rest, so help us, God, as we submit
ourselves to You. You are our Heavenly Father and we
will come home to you in Yeshua's name."

The End?...not really, just a new beginning!

Bibliography

1. Foote, John Taintor, Garrett Fort, Bess Meredyth, Johnston McCulley, *The Mark of Zorro*. Directed by Rouben Mamoulian. Los Angeles: Twentieth Century Fox Film Corporation, 1940. The Mark of Zorro.

2. Hitler, Adolf. (1971). *Mein kampf.* Boston & New York: Houghton Mifflin Company.

3. Wiener, Peter F. (1999). *Martin Luther: Hitler's spiritual ancestor.* Cranford, New Jersey: American Atheist Press.

4. Lash, Jamie. (1997). The ancient jewish wedding: And the return of Messiah for his bride. Jewish Jewels.

5. Fruchtebaum, Arnold. (2013 revised). *The Footsteps of the Messiah,* p.cm. Originally published: San Antonio, TX: Ariel Press c 1982.

6. Black, Claudia. (1981). *It'll Never Happen to Me.* (Chapter 3: Children of alcoholics: As youngsters adolescents – adults. USA, A Ballantine Book: The Random House Publishing Group.

7. Kerr, Michael E. *"One Family's Story: A Primer on Bowen Theory."* The Bowen Center for the Study of the Family. 2000. http://www.thebowencenter.org.

8. Alexander Pope, *An Essay on Criticism,* Part II, 1711.

9. Bradford, Wilcox W., Rosenberg et al. (2006). The importance of fathers in the healthy development of children. Child Abuse and Neglect User Manual Series, pages 11, 12, 13. Retrieved from https://www.childwelfare.gov/pubPDFs/fatherhood.pdf 2.

10. "In search of lost time. Why is everyone so busy?" The Economist. Retrieved February 17, 2017 from http://www.economist.com/news/christmas-specials/21636612-time-poverty-problem-partly-perception-and-partly-distribution-why.

11. Kreider, Tim, ANXIETY the 'busy' trap. *The New York Times.* Opinionator. Retrieved February 17, 2017 from https://opinionator.blogs.nytimes.com/2012/06/30/the-busy-trap.

12. The Aryeh Kaplan Series, Copyright 1974 Aryeh Kaplan, "Sabbath-Day of Eternity" New Edition Copyright 1982, 1993 (OU/NCSY Pg. 32).

We're here to help you arrive safely on your bold journey home!

We are all part of a grand story, a story bigger than our individual stories, and each of us plays a vital role. In fact, the grand story is incomplete without your story.

The ultimate goal of the Grand Story is to get you safely back home, but the long journey home is often anything but safe. It is typically filled with plenty of nail-biting twists and turns that will test your resolve. You may experience seasons of doubt, sadness, confusion, anger, and loneliness. And at times, you might even want to give up.

https://www.boldjourney.com

Gene Binder is a gifted speaker on a variety of subjects and has had the privilege of speaking to many churches, organizations and groups around the world. Gene's Jewish background, overcoming many serious life-challenges, and over thirty-years as a teaching pastor, afford deeper insights into the topics he teaches on.

- Faith Communities
- Leadership Teams
- Retreats
- Marriage retreats with his wife Andrea
- Conferences

For speaking inquiries contact Gene at:
genemichaelbinder@gmail.com

If you're a fan of this book, will you help me spread the word?

There are several ways you can help me get the word out about the message of this book…

- Post a 5-Star review on Amazon.

- Write about the book on your Facebook, Twitter and Instagram!

- If you blog, consider referencing the book, or publishing an excerpt from the book with a link back to my website.

- Recommend the book to friends—word of mouth is still the most effective form of advertising.

- Purchase additional copies to give away as gifts.